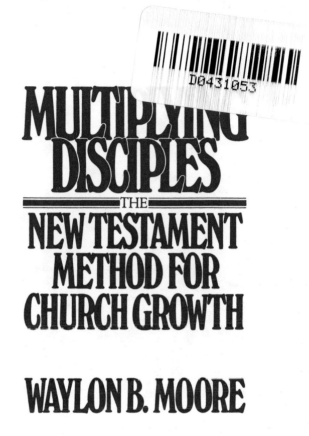

MULTIPLYING DISCIPLES

THE
NEW TESTAMENT METHOD FOR CHURCH GROWTH

WAYLON B. MOORE

NAVPRESS

A MINISTRY OF THE NAVIGATORS
P.O. Box 6000, Colorado Springs, Colorado 80934

The Navigators is an international, evangelical Christian organization. Jesus Christ gave his followers the Great Commission to go and make disciples (Matthew 28:19). The aim of The Navigators is to help fulfill that commission by multiplying laborers for Christ in every nation.

NavPress is the publishing ministry of The Navigators. NavPress publications are tools to help Christians grow. Although publications alone cannot make disciples or change lives, they can help believers learn biblical discipleship, and apply what they learn to their lives and ministries.

Scripture quotations are primarily from the *King James Version*. Another version used is the *New International Version* (NIV), © 1978 by the New York International Bible Society.

Printed in the United States of America

Contents

Foreword 5

Preface 7

Acknowledgments 11

PART ONE—

THE CHALLENGE: REACHING THE WORLD

  1 You Can Multiply Yourself Through Others 15

PART TWO—

THE METHOD: MULTIPLYING DISCIPLES

  2 The Meaning of Discipleship 21

  3 Why Build Disciples? 27

  4 Biblical Examples of Spiritual Multiplication 35

  5 Where Disciplemaking Begins 41

PART THREE—

THE PROCESS: HOW TO BUILD MULTIPLYING DISCIPLES

  6 Spiritual Qualities of the Multiplying Disciplemaker 51

  7 Have a Servant Heart 57

  8 Presence with the Disciple 67

  9 Have a Parent Heart 75

  10 Be a Pacesetter 91

PART FOUR—

THE PRACTICE: GETTING STARTED NOW

  11 Selecting Potential Multiplying Leaders 103

  12 Begin in Your Church Today 111

  13 Anyone Can Multiply 121

Appendix 127

Foreword

A few years ago I was in a large church in Florida for a series of meetings. It was no ordinary church. The immediate counseling done with new converts was the most thorough I had ever seen. A class for new members was the most effective I had ever observed. Above all, there was a group of laymen who were equipped as competent spiritual leaders. These men assumed the major task of equipping others. The pastor of that church was the author of this book, Waylon Moore.

Waylon is one of the pioneers in the contemporary discipleship movement which gives wholesome emphasis to follow-up and thorough one-on-one training of spiritual leaders. This book conveys the spirit of the author who has carried the vision of multiplying disciples not only to this land but to many countries of our world.

Perhaps the strongest feature of *Multiplying Disciples* is its obvious biblical basis. As would be expected, a biblically based book on this subject should have a right blending of evangelism and discipleship. This book magnifies both. The author writes, "When the church exhales disciples, it inhales converts." To Waylon, the goal of discipling is the development of a committed group of believers who will effectively penetrate a lost world. The book also strongly links the ministry of disciple-making to the local church.

Books about discipleship must be written by practitioners. This splendid book is written by a man who for many years has practiced what he writes. His objective is to create vision and action in the life of a reader toward the ministries of evangelism, follow-up, and leadership training. This book will be an extremely useful tool for anybody who is committed to fully obeying the Great Commission.

Roy J. Fish
Professor of Evangelism
Southwestern Baptist Theological
  Seminary
Fort Worth, Texas

Preface

A new breath of the Spirit is working in hearts across North America and in many nations around the world. New patterns of ministry are being tried with growing success. Never in the history of the Church have more people professed faith in Christ than in this century.

However, the quality of spiritual life in the local church is unfortunately still open to question at a time when millions hunger to experience the fullness of life in Christ.

In contemporary society, the supreme worth of the individual has been rediscovered politically and socially. Minority groups have gained new freedoms. Church leaders everywhere are beginning to see vast potential in small group approaches, and especially in one-on-one discipling, for effective spiritual multiplication.

Three challenges confront those who have a heart for evangelism and church growth.

First, there must be a radical commitment to validating conversion experience through the counseling of all new members entering the local church. Too many individuals without a vital spiritual life are packing pews for what has sadly become a kind of post-Christian memorial service.

Second, there must be a renewed commitment to the responsible follow-up and integration of all those new members into a living fellowship within the local church. It is essential that these new members be given the kind of help which will lead them personally into regular self-feeding habits of quiet time, Bible study, and witnessing to their faith.

Third, each church must commit itself to responsible

long-range leadership training through discipleship ministries to produce spiritual multipliers capable of building other "laborers for the harvest."

Veteran missionaries from three continents have told me, "We are twenty to forty years behind in leadership training. We can't keep up with the current explosion of new believers. Leaders who can instruct these groups of new Christians simply can't be produced fast enough through present methods in our seminaries and Bible institutes."

If a pastor or missionary begins an individual, one-on-one ministry with one or two disciples, however, the process of multiplication can take place quite rapidly. Unfortunately, the majority of the training approaches in use today revolve around the classroom, the group, or the congregation. Balancing these larger training classes with one-on-one time is desperately needed. Discipling others is nothing less than the investment of one's life: to "lay down our lives for the brethren" (1 John 3:16) simply can't be packed into a formal one-on-one, two-hour session during the week.

In my first book, *New Testament Follow-Up*, I shared some practical and tested scriptural concepts for initiating counseling and follow-up in the local church.

This book deals with how to establish long-range leadership training in order to produce carefully discipled multipliers capable of building still more "laborers for the harvest."

Seeing biblical principles of spiritual multiplication applied in some churches has encouraged me to share the principles with a wider audience. Three things are at the core of multiplication: interceding with God for another disciple, helping him grow to his full potential in Christ, and being available to him. Nothing I've done in thirty years of ministry compares with the effectiveness of this kind of personal commitment to helping another individual become the best he can be in Christ. May I commend this book to those of you who wish to multiply disciples in your local church.

Waylon B. Moore
Tampa, Florida

Acknowledgments

My special thanks to my wife, Clemmie, who never stopped encouraging me, to Avery and Steve who believed, and to those friends who stood with us faithfully through the years. Thanks also to Monte Unger for his skillful editing, and to David Tucker who helped me express my ideas graphically.

The sources for the quotations found on the following pages are listed below.

page 15 - *Goforth of China*
page 21 - *The Quotable Billy Graham*
page 51 - *The Incredible Christian*
page 57 - *A New Heaven*
page 75 - *Choosing and Changing*
page 91 - *Master Plan of Evangelism*

PART ONE

The Challenge: Reaching the World

CHAPTER ONE

You Can Multiply Yourself Through Others

*"All of God's
giants have been
weak men who
did great things for
God because they
reckoned on God
being with them"*
—Hudson Taylor

YOU CAN BEGIN spiritually multiplying yourself today, and start a dynamic process which could reach beyond your generation and into the next century. This would be your part in accomplishing Christ's Great Commission to go into all the world and make disciples (see Matthew 28:18-20). That is what this book is all about: *spiritual multiplication through the process of disciplemaking, with the ultimate objective of reaching the world for Christ.* This is something anyone can do anywhere, but the best place to start is in your local church.

Consider the example of a Sunday school teacher in the 1800s named Edward Kimball, who began making disciples in his class. The results are with us right now in the 1980s. In fact, you may even be a direct result of Kimball's spiritual multiplication.

Edward Kimball was committed to reaching every lost youth in his Sunday school class. He was particularly burdened for one backward fellow, fresh from the farmlands, who had begun working in a nearby shoe shop. One day Kimball went to the shop and, in the back room, persuaded the young man to accept Christ as his personal Savior.

When describing the youth, Kimball said, "I have seen few persons whose minds were spiritually darker when he came into my Sunday school class, or one who seemed more unlikely ever to become a Christian of clear decided views, still less to fill any sphere of extended public usefulness."[1] But the young man, Dwight L. Moody, went on to become known as a pioneer in modern techniques of mass evangelism and as a Spirit-anointed preacher whose message touched millions in North America and Europe.

Actually, it was during Moody's crusades in England when Kimball's chain of spiritual multiplication was mightily carried forward. More than one English pastor rejected the fiery visitor's approach to evangelism. One of them, the Reverend F. B. Meyer, was not taken at all with the crudeness of the unlettered, blunt evangelist. Yet even his heart melted when he heard two ladies, both Sunday school teachers in his own church, tell how they had been influenced by Moody's commitment to win all of the members of his own Sunday school class to Christ.

Those two women did reach all the members in their classes. Renewed by the Holy Spirit through the commitment of these women, Meyer joined in Moody's evangelistic meetings with wholehearted enthusiasm.

Moody later invited Meyer to the United States. Among those reached by Meyer's Bible teaching ministry was a struggling young preacher named J. Wilber Chapman, whose approach was so transformed that he, too, went into an evangelistic ministry.

Though he was used by God all over the world in bringing people to Christ, it was Chapman's own crusade advance man, a former clerk in the Young Men's Christian Association, who was to carry on Kimball's chain of multiplication. His name was Billy Sunday.

Sunday preached across North America with spectacular results. His crusade in Charlotte, North Carolina, produced some converts who organized a prayer group that met for years, praying that God would continue the ministry of evangelism through the people of Charlotte. This group of praying men was led by the Holy Spirit to plan a city-wide crusade. They invited Mordecai Ham, the cowboy evangelist, to speak. During one meeting, some teenagers were among those reached for Christ. They included a young man named Billy Graham.

Only heaven will reveal the actual number of people reached through the chain of multiplying disciples as a result of Edward Kimball's humble efforts in the 1800s in his local church.

Christ calls us to be disciples who will multiply spiritually. Multiplication should be the result of conscious application of biblical principles, not just coincidence. Whether you're a lay man or woman, pastor, or other Christian worker, this book is written to help you multiply yourself through many future generations by making disciples. This ministry will last through all eternity as you invest in the lives of individuals who will, in turn, reach others . . . who will reach others . . . who will reach others.

You can start in your church today!

QUESTIONS FOR STUDY AND DISCUSSION

1. How often do you see others being influenced for

Christ as the result of a carefully designed plan? Discuss some examples of spiritual multiplication from your own experience, observation, or reading.

========================NOTES========================

1. A. P. Fitt, *The Life of D. L. Moody* (Chicago: Moody Press, n.d.), page 23.

PART TWO

The Method:
Multiplying Disciples

CHAPTER TWO

The Meaning of Discipleship

*"Salvation is free,
but discipleship
costs everything
we have"*
—Billy Graham

DISCIPLE WAS CHRIST'S favorite word for those whose lives were intricately linked with his. The Greek word for disciple, *mathetes*, is used 269 times in the Gospels and Acts. It means a "taught" or "trained" one.

In the Gospel of John, Jesus defines the word *disciple* in three ways.

First, *a disciple is a Christian who is involved in the word of God on a continual basis.* "Then said Jesus to those Jews which believed on him, If ye continue in my word, then are ye my disciples indeed" (John 8:31). The Bible is much more than a mere book; it is a reliable guide for daily living. The continual application of Scripture results in learning the truths which, according to Jesus, set one free (see John 8:32).

Second, *a disciple is one who lays down his life for others.*

"A new commandment I give unto you, that ye love one another; as I have loved you, that ye also love one another. By this shall all men know that ye are my disciples, if ye have love one to another" (John 13:34-35).

But what kind of love is this? It is far more than merely doing a few good deeds. In John 15:13, Jesus says, "Greater love hath no man than this, that a man lay down his life for his friends." This gives love a far deeper meaning: a disciple loves enough to be unpopular, to be misunderstood, to stand alone, to suffer. Love is unconditional.

Jesus captured the hearts of his disciples with his unconditional love. His love always sought to do what was best for those he trained. To love our brothers we must sacrifice for their deepest needs. As John, the beloved disciple, wrote, "Hereby perceive we the love of God, because he laid down his life for us: and we ought to lay down our lives for the brethren" (1 John 3:16). Jesus defines discipleship in part as loving other believers. Men can see Christ in our lives only when they see us loving one another.

But this is an uncommon love. By "laying down our lives" for others, we die to certain things. We give up certain rights. We may have to sacrifice money, time, and possessions in order to love others better. This is possible in our churches today as "the love of God is shed abroad in our hearts by the Holy Ghost" (Romans 5:5).

Third, *a disciple is one who abides daily in a fruit-bearing union with Christ.* Jesus said,

Abide in me, and I in you. As the branch cannot bear fruit of itself, except it abide in the vine; no more can ye, except ye abide in me. I am the vine, ye are the branches: He that abideth in me, and I in him, the same bringeth forth much fruit: *for without me ye can do nothing* (John 15:4-5, italics mine).

22

The word *fruit* is used several ways in the Scriptures. This passage seems to be more illustrative of the fruit of our union with Christ, rather than the fruit of the Spirit as explained in Galatians 5:22-23. This is further discussed in John 15:8: "Herein is my Father glorified, that ye bear much fruit; so shall ye be my disciples."

So Christ's disciples are those who bear fruit that comes from abiding in union with him. Christ's prayer for the disciples recorded in John 17 shows that the fruit mentioned in John 15 is *people*: "Neither pray I for these alone, but for them also which shall believe on me through their word" (John 17:20).

Jesus emphasized lasting fruit in his teaching: "Ye have not chosen me, but I have chosen you, and ordained you, that ye should go and bring forth fruit, and that your fruit should remain: that whatsoever ye shall ask of the Father in my name, he may give it you" (John 15:16).

Our union with Christ makes possible a life through which others can be saved. When a tree is so full of sap that it can no longer hold it, the result is fruit! When a Christian is full of Christ, others see him and hear about him and are then spiritually reborn into the kingdom of God. Thus, new believers are one fruit of true discipleship. By merely sitting still, one can have the inward fruit of the Spirit, but Jesus says we are also to "go and bring forth fruit."

"The harvest truly is plenteous, but the labourers are few; pray ye therefore the Lord of the harvest, that he will send forth labourers into his harvest" (Matthew 9:37-38). The world desperately needs laborers (disciples), men and women who are abiding in Christ, obeying and applying the Scriptures daily, evangelizing the lost effectively, and reaching out in Christlike love to their brothers and sisters in the church. Thus, we can help to reach the world—that great, ripe harvest field!

23

CONDITIONS OF DISCIPLESHIP

Jesus enlarges on the concept of discipleship in Luke 14 with some specific, practical conditions for those who follow him. In Luke 14:26 he talks about our loving him more than father, mother, or family. He also equates discipleship with an unrivaled love for him even above one's own life. "And whosoever doth not bear his cross, and come after me, cannot be my disciple" (Luke 14:27).

Do you want to be his disciple? Then you have to bear the cross. This is the instrument of death to self we are to take up each day. True discipleship calls for an attitude of commitment to the revealed will of God—one which views everything that comes our way as something sent from his hands. Rather than clinging tightly to earthly things, we should be willing to drop them (bear the cross) for his cause.

Paul, the Christ-centered missionary, understood that there must be a commitment to Jesus who bought the right to be our Lord with his own blood: "And that he died for all, that they which live should not henceforth live unto themselves, but unto him which died for them, and rose again" (2 Corinthians 5:15). Christ must have preeminence in our lives and ministries.

A. W. Tozer said there are three characteristics of one crucified with Christ: "He has no plans of his own, he is looking only in one direction, and he isn't coming down."[1]

If we want to enjoy an exciting, living relationship with Christ daily, we must be willing to pay a price; personal discipline will be required. There may be loneliness. There may be a lack of popularity as we progress from the death of our dreams and plans towards the glorious resurrection of living through his indwelling life. Many Christians move toward the goal of cross-bearing in their identification with Christ, but quit too soon. "Demas hath forsaken me, having loved this present world" (2 Timothy 4:10), wrote Paul about a disciple who started the journey but gave it up too early.

Christ insists that he must be our exclusive focus in life. "So likewise, whosoever he be of you that forsaketh not all that he hath, he cannot be my disciple" (Luke 14:33). Making an irrevocable commitment to Christ as Lord is essential for biblical discipleship, but it is not enough. This commitment must be renewed daily.

Reevaluate your walk with Christ in the light of these scriptural definitions of discipleship, for before you can disciple others, you must first be a disciple yourself.

QUESTIONS FOR STUDY AND DISCUSSION

1. In your own words, state the three definitions of a disciple given by Jesus in John's Gospel.
2. How would you summarize Jesus' emphasis in Luke 14:26-34 on discipleship as total surrender?
3. Name a few of the qualities that you think should characterize a modern disciple of Christ.
4. Discuss the relationship of following Christ in Luke 14 to the recovery of valuables in Luke 15.
5. Discuss the concept that "every saved person is Christ's disciple" as it relates to the definition of Christ's disciples ("those who meet the biblical qualifications outlined in the Gospels").

═══════════════NOTES═══════════════

1. A. W. Tozer, from a lecture at Christian Missionary Alliance Church, Chicago, Illinois, 1957.

CHAPTER THREE

Why Build Disciples?

"Would you spend as much time preparing yourself to meet the needs of one person as you would preparing a sermon for five thousand? How much do you believe in the potential of one?"
—K. Bruce Miller

THERE ARE AT least three major biblical precedents for building disciples—the use of discipling in the Old Testament, and Jesus' public and private ministries.

OLD TESTAMENT DISCIPLING

The concept of sharing with another what God is sharing with you is centuries old. Moses opened his heart and life to Joshua. But the sharing approach wasn't a natural idea for Moses. God set a pattern for instruction by *commanding* Moses to share his life with Joshua in Deuteronomy 3:28: "But charge Joshua, and encourage him, and strengthen him: for he shall go over before this people."

Moses was to pour into his apprentice, Joshua, all that God was teaching him. This meant giving Joshua much personal time in which he would learn by observation and conversation. God's servant Moses became a human channel for developing Joshua into a servant of God.

Why would God have to command Moses to break away from a pattern of ministry to the thousands to touch just a single life? Because it is man's natural tendency to see the needs of the many *en masse*, rather than to see the potential in a single life surrendered to God's total will. As Sam Shoemaker once said, "Men are not hewn out of the mediocre mass wholesale, but one by one."[1]

Elijah, too, had disciples, in a school for young prophets. Through this band of men, God would work to bring either revival or judgment to Israel. Among them was Elisha, a like-hearted young man. Amazingly, Elisha asked Elijah for a double portion of his power with God. He had seen the miracle and might of God through the strong arm of Elijah. Through discipline and vision sharing, Elisha had learned to ask bold things of God.

There are other Old Testament examples of one person investing his life in another's: David with his mighty men; the patriarchs' training of their children; and the concrete commands to fathers to teach their children who would in turn teach their own (see Deuteronomy 4:9 and 6:6-7). This teacher-pupil emphasis laid a foundation for the ministry of discipling in the New Testament.

JESUS' PUBLIC MINISTRY

Jesus had a broad public ministry, involving four basic approaches.

He preached. The multitudes heard of the kingdom, of

judgment on religious hypocrisy, and of the nature of God through Jesus' preaching. He brought new revelation to Old Testament concepts buried in tradition. He revealed the ultimate truth beyond legalism. "The common people heard him gladly" (Mark 12:37) as he preached with love and authority.

He taught. He taught as no man had ever taught—to the multitudes on a hillside overlooking the Sea of Galilee, to groups in villages, to individuals in the privacy of their homes, to the curious, and to the committed. He revealed truth in its raw purity through parables that illuminated the reality of life. It is not surprising that he used all ten methods of teaching catalogued by modern scholars.[2]

He healed. No one ever left Jesus' presence still wanting wholeness. On one occasion, many people gathered around him, "And the whole multitude sought to touch him: for there went virtue out of him, and healed them all" (Luke 6:19). A world without hospitals and medical insurance found the Great Physician and sought never to let him go.

He performed miracles. The crowds hovered about and followed as the Master healed the leper, gave sight to the blind, fed multitudes, and raised the dead. His disciples were awed when he calmed the storm. In the stillness that followed, they saw Jesus walking on the water through the mists toward their boat.

Historically, the Christian Church has embraced each of these aspects of Christ's public ministry, but it has often neglected the examples set by Christ in his private ministry.

JESUS' PRIVATE MINISTRY

Jesus also had a strategic private ministry that was so simple that it has been overlooked as a principle of Church mission.

29

The compelling commitment of Christ was to build disciples who would multiply the message of his life, death, and resurrection to all nations. He said,

> All authority in heaven and on earth has been given to me. Therefore go and make disciples of all nations, baptizing them in the name of the Father and of the Son and of the Holy Spirit, and teaching them to obey everything I have commanded you (Matthew 28:18-20, NIV).

If we are to copy Jesus' total ministry, then the Church must reach out both in evangelism and in the establishing of converts. As the converts grow, they, too, can be taught how to equip and train other believers who in turn will reach others through the process of spiritual multiplication.

Soul-winning is not disciplemaking, but soul-winning is vital if the disciples are going to be able to reproduce themselves in the lives of others. Evangelism is the first link in the chain of spiritual multiplication.

Churches with an overemphasis on baptisms and programs, or an undue concern for "quality membership," must reconsider Christ's command to make disciples. Saving souls and building disciples are inseparably linked in Scripture.

DISCIPLEMAKING IS A WORKABLE METHOD

In reviewing my motivation to disciple others, I remember how someone cared for me—and how that loving care and the subsequent flow into my life of what he had learned from God changed my life. Disciplemaking has no prestige rating, no denominational category; but the results are consistently better than anything I have experienced in thirty years of working with people. There are several reasons.

Discipling is one of the most strategic ways to have an unlimited personal ministry. It may be done at any time, by anyone, anywhere, and among any age group.

Discipling is the most flexible of ministries. Since it need not be done within any time frame or organizational structure, the disciplemaker can be extremely flexible.

Discipling is the fastest and surest way to mobilize the whole body of Christ for evangelism. The goal of discipling is not just more disciples, for a club comprised of saved souls will soon die without effective penetration into the lost world. One of the fastest ways to increase baptisms and deepen the quality of life of those reached for Christ is through discipling. Making disciples in all nations becomes both a result of evangelizing and a means to the accomplishment of world evangelization.

Discipling has more long-range potential for fruit than any other ministry. The Lord wants us to be rooted and built up in him and established in the faith (see Colossians 2:7). This takes time and care. Caring for people is the essential component. Follow-up is done by some*one* rather than some*thing*.

Discipling will provide the local church with mature lay leaders who are Christ-centered and word-oriented. The pew warmers are many; the laborers are few. Laborers are a product of Spirit-guided discipling in the church. Building into the lives of others is God's plan for raising up new deacons, teachers, and other church leaders. The nominating committee's appeal for workers will become a shout of praise to God when church members are multiplying Christ-like disciples.

THE CYCLE OF LEADERSHIP

As we have just seen, building disciples develops the future leaders of the church. How then can we accelerate leadership training in order to be prepared for the future?

Evangelism is the means to making converts and the training ground for developing disciples. When the church exhales disciples, it inhales converts; thus, the church grows. Discipleship is the fastest way to multiply leaders who will expedite both evangelism and discipleship.

My illustration of the "Cycle of Leadership" in the local church (see Figure A on page 33) may help you understand the multiplication of leaders. The figure is intended not as a black and white categorization of people in the church, but as a representation of levels of growth within the church.

Through follow-up the convert is loved, fed, protected, and trained (see chapter five). He becomes a disciple, a growing follower of Christ. As the disciple receives individual training (by a more mature disciple), he becomes able to multiply. A multiplier has trained one or more disciples who have reached another. A builder of multipliers trains other multipliers.

The discipling process is represented by the arrows going down—as each leader develops growing disciples. The cycle is completed and begins again as each convert grows to his full potential in the likeness of Christ, represented by the arrows pointing towards the builder. The arrows reaching out into a lost world represent church evangelism by all who are Spirit-led converts, disciples, multipliers, and builders.

This cycle of leadership is a visual concept of church growth through receiving training for the task and reaching out to the unsaved. Through a person-to-person ministry, the multipliers (the first generation) advise, encourage, and sharpen disciples (second generation). In a few weeks or months, God develops a team of witnesses. They visit friends, relatives, neighbors, or job contacts, and some people are born again. When these second generation disciples have won converts (third generation), multiplication has begun.

CYCLE OF LEADERSHIP

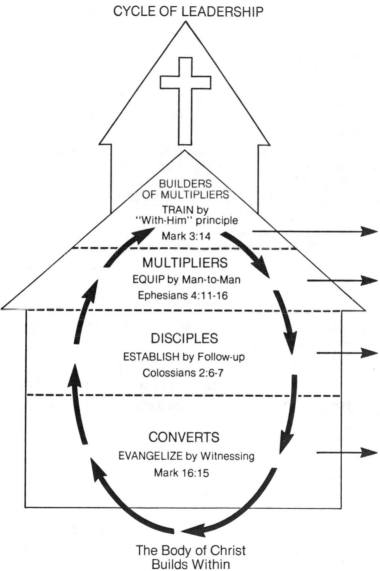

BUILDERS
OF MULTIPLIERS
TRAIN by
"With-Him" principle
Mark 3:14

MULTIPLIERS
EQUIP by Man-to-Man
Ephesians 4:11-16

DISCIPLES
ESTABLISH by Follow-up
Colossians 2:6-7

CONVERTS
EVANGELIZE by Witnessing
Mark 16:15

The Body of Christ
Builds Within

Figure A

QUESTIONS FOR STUDY AND DISCUSSION

1. In relation to your church's ministry, discuss Christ's concentration on four basic approaches to ministry.

2. Has your church made a commitment to emulate Jesus' private discipling ministry? What would you suggest for a stronger union of the public and private ministries in your church?

3. What place should Sunday school, church training, and youth ministries have in the private ministry of discipling? What strengths and weaknesses are apparent in the public and private ministry approaches used throughout the Bible?

4. How could you make a commitment to practicing discipleship modeled on Jesus' private ministry?

5. What reasons for discipling another person are most important to you? Why?

6. Discuss some other advantages of discipling.

7. Discuss the "Cycle of Leadership" illustration from your church's viewpoint.
   a) How many in your church are converts, disciples, multipliers, and builders of multipliers?
   b) Why is evangelism essential in each part of the cycle?

8. How could you either initiate a discipling ministry in your church, or strengthen the current emphasis on discipleship training?

===================== NOTES =====================

1. Sam Shoemaker, *Revive Thy Church Beginning with Me* (New York: Harper Brothers, 1948), page 112.

2. F. H. Roberts, Master's Thesis, Dallas Seminary, 1955, pages iii-iv.

CHAPTER FOUR

Biblical Examples of Spiritual Multiplication

"For who hath despised the day of small things?"
(Zechariah 4:10)

IT IS DIFFICULT for us to identify with the giant builders of multipliers like Paul and Peter. Few of us will exercise such mighty authority and spiritual power as did Paul. Fewer still will preach as Peter did and see three thousand saved at one service. But we must not let this discourage us, for there are men and women in the Bible we can identify with in our personal disciplemaking.

ANDREW

In the Gospels, Andrew was always bringing people to Jesus. He brought his brother, Simon (see John 1:40-42); this Simon became the giant of the faith, Peter. Andrew found the boy whose small lunch Jesus multiplied to feed the five thousand (see John 6:8-9). And when the Greeks said, "Sir, we would see Jesus," Andrew knew where to take them (John 12:21).

It was by reaching his brother Peter, however, that Andrew's ministry extended even into our day. At Pentecost, Peter evangelized thousands of Jews who trusted Christ (see Acts 2). Those converted in Jerusalem eventually left because of persecution (see Acts 8:1-4) and traveled to Antioch (see Acts 11:19), where other Jews were converted through their personal evangelism. As Peter grew in grace after the resurrection, God empowered him to open the door for the conversion of the Gentiles when Cornelius and his household believed (see Acts 10).

This is multiplication; from Andrew, to Peter, to the thousands converted in Jerusalem, to the first mission church at Antioch. Andrew did his preaching by personal evangelism; he brought people to Jesus one by one. By bringing his brother Peter to Christ, Andrew shared the rewards of everything Simon Peter eventually accomplished for God's kingdom.

This is how you can expand your ministry around the world—by reaching just one other person who may multiply mightily.

JOHN

The apostle John trained men: his three letters to church leaders reveal his continuing responsibility as a spiritual father. Church history records that John won and trained a dynamic witness named Polycarp, who in turn reached and discipled Irenaeus, who became a pastor. These men gave their lives during persecutions in the second century. However, through multiplication, their ministry lived on.

BARNABAS

In Acts 4 we meet a Christian named Joses, a man close enough to the apostles to be renamed "Barnabas, the encourager." What a man! He heard the testimony of a young convert named Saul of Tarsus and believed it was genuine.

Barnabas always looked past peoples' problems to the potential he saw by the work of God's grace. When Saul traveled to Jerusalem, everyone was afraid of him. Barnabas, however, affirmed Saul before the brethren. Later they were together for a year of man-to-man ministry at Antioch (see Acts 11:22-26). Paul had already been privately taught by the Holy Spirit for three years in the desert. But God used Barnabas to encourage, refine, and strengthen this multi-gifted rabbi whom others would not touch.

Barnabas made a commitment to disciple his nephew, John Mark. When Mark quit the first missionary journey, Paul refused to allow him a second chance. In the division with Barnabas over Mark, Paul chose Silas and Timothy and walked into history. Barnabas stuck with Mark. However, in 2 Timothy 4:11 (NIV), when Paul asks Timothy for his books and cloak, he also writes, "Get Mark and bring him with you, because he is helpful to me in my ministry."

What transforms a quitter into a helper? Certainly we cannot evaluate Mark apart from the personal time, love, and training he received from both Peter and Barnabas. God used these multipliers to develop those qualities in Mark which were hidden from Paul's observation of him.

AQUILA AND PRISCILLA

Paul began another multiplication chain when he met Aquila and Priscilla. This couple followed up and discipled a man named Apollos (see Acts 18:24-28). The Jews were "mightily convicted" through the teaching ministry of Apollos. God formed a four-generation chain of spiritual multiplication from Paul to Aquila and Priscilla, then to Apollos, and finally to the Jews.

Paul reached many others in a personal way who went on to have an impact on history, including Luke. Luke went on to write both his Gospel and the book of Acts to follow up one man, Theophilus (see Luke 1:1-4 and Acts 1:1). Titus, another in Paul's ministry, eventually pastored a church in Crete.

YOU CAN MULTIPLY YOURSELF

Consider the "Chain of Multiplication," Figure B, which shows spiritual reproduction in the New Testament.

CHAIN OF MULTIPLICATION

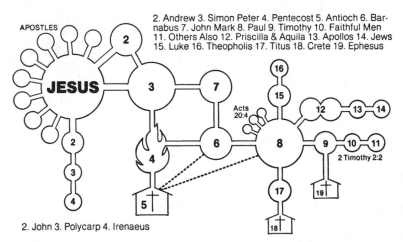

2. Andrew 3. Simon Peter 4. Pentecost 5. Antioch 6. Barnabus 7. John Mark 8. Paul 9. Timothy 10. Faithful Men 11. Others Also 12. Priscilla & Aquila 13. Apollos 14. Jews 15. Luke 16. Theopholis 17. Titus 18. Crete 19. Ephesus

2. John 3. Polycarp 4. Irenaeus

Figure B

Neither Andrew nor Barnabas were as gifted as the ones they reached. However, both men shared lovingly with others what they knew of Christ. And both had a part in the spiritual rewards of those they helped.

We can be encouraged by the examples of Andrew and Barnabas and realize that each of us is able to make disciples and multiply. God wants to give us a potential Peter or Paul or Timothy. Availability to the Spirit's guidance is essential if we are to multiply. You can be an Andrew.

QUESTIONS FOR STUDY AND DISCUSSION

1. Recall the "Andrews" who were responsible for bringing you to Christ. Do you know anything about the chain of multiplication that brought them to Christ?

2. Who has played the part of a Barnabas in your life by encouraging you either as a new Christian or in some recent decision?

3. From the passages in Acts 9, 11, and 15, how easy or difficult do you think Barnabas's discipling of Paul was?

4. What kind of person could God use to start a multiplication chain in your church? Specify some of the qualities you have observed in Andrew's or Barnabas's life.

CHAPTER FIVE

Where Disciplemaking Begins

*"Decision is five
percent; following
up the decision is
the ninety-five
percent"*
—Billy Graham

EVERY BORN-AGAIN person is a miracle of God's grace. It is in God's plan that each miraculous new life grow into the fullness of Christ. A healthy spiritual birth is essential to growth in discipleship. Some spiritual retardation in church members can be traced to unclear initial decisions for Christ. The implementation of Paul's methods of caring for new believers will enable the local church to strengthen new Christians immediately for responsible discipleship.

The new believer is a spiritual child, and must have immediate parental care. The shockingly long time that is often allowed to pass between decision and initial follow-up is a major negative factor that hinders future growth. *Within twenty-four hours* the convert should be prayed for, personally contacted, and shown how to begin feeding on the word of God. A baby needs loving care and food! When we remember the three years of *daily* discipling by Jesus and Paul's years of fellowship with Timothy and Titus, we see that follow-up is not solved by one or two church services.

THE BAPTISM GAP

In the United States, pastors have indicated that up to 50 percent of those making decisions in their churches are not baptized afterward. In South America some pastors have said that eight out of ten of those who make a decision for Christ in an evangelistic meeting never come back to the church. The same thing is happening in Africa and Asia.

There are heartbreaking gaps between the hundreds of professions of faith in the churches and the dozens of people who are actually baptized, effectively integrated into the life of the local church, and growing in Christ a year later.

Although there are many reasons why churches lose so many new converts (such as an unclear gospel presentation or decisions based on peer pressure), the major loss is the result of an inadequate understanding and philosophy of the follow-up principles given to us in the New Testament.

Immediate counseling is essential. (For help in establishing a total church follow-up ministry, consult some of the available books on the subject.)[1]

FOUR METHODS OF FOLLOW-UP FROM 1 THESSALONIANS

In the first century A.D., how were the apostles and evangelists able to transform a small group of uneducated people into vibrant disciples who revolutionized the Roman world within a few hundred years? We know that the gospel had penetrated the known world within about thirty-three years after the resurrection. It had been done without the printing press, telephone, television, or Tel-Star. The believers used "tell-a-man" and "tell-a-woman." Something had been done *with* the new converts that dynamically changed their lives in the midst of the fleshpots of the ancient world. New Christians growing in Christ became church fellowships, and the young churches multiplied!

First Thessalonians was one of the first New Testament epistles to be written, and it has as much in it on initial follow-up as any book other than the four Gospels. Here is what Paul teaches in 1 Thessalonians.

Personal Correspondence
Paul followed up new believers with personal letters (see 1 Thessalonians 1:1). Most of the New Testament is a series of personal letters to follow up the individual members of the various new churches. How can we use this concept today?

Personal letters, coupled with simple, one-page Bible studies, are good spiritual food for the nourishment of new believers. The studies should be simple, systematic, personally applicable, easily passed on, and should involve the new Christian in *writing down* his answers.

Even a form letter, sent to all of the new believers in your church to explain some of the principles of the new life in Christ—victory over temptation, forgiveness, how to have a quiet time, and how to witness—can reap major dividends. The longer a convert takes to begin growing, the less likely it is that he will mature fully, and the less time he will have left to devote to ministering to others.

Peter and John wrote letters to follow up those from whom they were separated. And without Paul's imprisonments, we might not have one fourth of the New Testament. One of the blessings of those "lost years" in prison was the richness of some of the most widely read New Testament books, the letters Paul wrote to help new believers grow.

Toby was a fine young teenager who attended my first country church. He was spiritually sensitive and hungry to grow in the Lord. When I took a pastorate in another city, I began writing to Toby regularly, encouraging him in the basics of Christian living. I encouraged him to consider going to college. He did, and has since earned a doctorate and become a university professor.

Recently, in one of Toby's letters to me, he enclosed photocopies of all the letters I had written to him twenty-five years ago! How stumbling some of them were, yet Toby thanked me for caring, and kept all of them in spite of those imperfections of style.

Think of a letter that you received at some critical point in your life. Recall the supernatural way God used a caring heart miles away to reach into your life and bring change. Someone ministered to you by mail.

There are letters within each of us that need to be written to lift and strengthen others. Letter writing is a major ministry available to anyone, including the aged or infirm.

Personal Intercession
Paul's letters to the new churches reveal the importance he placed on personal intercession. He reminded the Thessalonians, "We give thanks to God always for you all, making mention of you in our prayers" (1 Thessalonians 1:2). Paul also described those prayers: "Night and day praying exceedingly that we might see your face, and might perfect that which is lacking in your faith" (1 Thessalonians 3:10).

In Ephesians 3:13-14, Paul writes, "Wherefore I desire that ye faint not at my tribulations for you . . . for this cause I bow my knees." Do you know anyone who is fainting spiritually? Intercession strengthens. When we don't pray for new believers, they will faint and drop out—sometimes permanently. If we don't pray, we will faint too (see Luke 18:1). Act on James's declaration that "the effectual fervent prayer of a righteous man availeth much" (James 5:16).

How and when should you intercede for new believers? Pray when you see someone baptized; otherwise it might be the last time you'll ever see him. At prayer services list the names of all the new believers on a blackboard and pray for them. Ask for volunteers who will adopt each new Christian for personal intercessory prayer during the week.

Most of us are where we are spiritually because someone prayed for us in faith. In Romans 16 Paul lists the names of at least twenty-eight individuals or families. How did he know so many people? Perhaps this roll call of the faithful in a far-off mission station reflects his own prayer list. We catch the spirit of his intercessory burden through the words "night and day" which appear in a number of Paul's letters. At the end of a long list of hardships which he gladly bears for Christ, he writes, "Beside those things that are without, that which cometh upon me daily, the care of all the churches" (2 Corinthians 11:28). Encourage memorization of Paul's prayers, for they are excellent examples of the kinds of requests which God answers to multiply his disciples and churches around the world.

Personal Representatives
Paul often helped new believers by sending a representative—someone he had personally trained to minister to them. In 1 Thessalonians 3:1-5, Timothy was sent to minister because Paul could not go. Epaphroditus, Titus, and others also were sent occasionally in Paul's place.

Paul sent "like-minded" men—men who were stamped with the same conviction and drive as their trainer. Of Timothy, Paul explained, "As a son with the father, he hath served with me in the gospel" (Philippians 2:22). How many like-minded men have you trained who could do your job if you couldn't go?

Personal Contact
Tender loving care by a more mature believer is an essential need of every convert. Letters are good, prayer is important, and so are personal representatives; but nothing replaces personal contact. Satan knows this and is committed to stopping regular church visitation. He twice stopped Paul's returning to visit the new believers in Thessalonica (see 1 Thessalonians 2:18).

Experience bears out the importance of personal contact. Most of the church members I've talked to about their growth into leadership in the church point to one or two people whose spiritual lives helped bring Christ into sharp focus for them. When a hungry heart sees Christ in another person, he is encouraged to keep growing in Christ.

Paul set a good pattern: he never preached and ran. Although "three Sabbath days" are mentioned specifically, some scholars believe Paul spent about three months in Thessalonica, and during that time gave hundreds of hours to the converts. He also worked, making tents to support the team of men who were with him. Is it any wonder that Thessalonica became an amazing, evangelistic missionary church (see 1 Thessalonians 1:7-9)? Nowhere in Scripture is there a stronger or more expressive description of person-to-person discipling than Paul's reference to sharing with the Thessalonians as their spiritual mother and father (see 1 Thessalonians 2:7 and 11). A more literal expression of verse eleven could be, "As you know how we were with you one by one, like a father with his own children, exhorting, calling, and witnessing." The vision and tone of Paul's parent heart is clearly communicated.

As Paul's example suggests, group dynamics and meetings are essential to help a convert grow into discipleship, but individual personal time will produce stronger and more lasting disciples. Most spiritual babes have problems that can only be solved on a private, individual basis.

Discipling, then, is done by someone, not by something. Literature is a good tool, but it is only that. God ultimately uses flesh and blood filled with the Holy Spirit to build lives (see 2 Corinthians 4:7).

QUESTIONS FOR STUDY AND DISCUSSION

1. What are some of the gaps left by the usual process of bringing a new Christian into the life of the church?

2. What could be done to welcome new believers and orient them to the congregation in ways that will insure continuing spiritual growth and development?

3. Discuss some of the ways a convert could be linked with a growing disciple in your church.

4. What were Paul's four methods for follow-up of new believers as mentioned in 1 Thessalonians?

5. Which of the four methods is already a functioning part of your church's ministry?

6. How could your church become more actively involved in applying each of these four biblical methods of follow-up this year?

NOTES

1. For example—Hal Brooks, *Follow-up Evangelism* (Nashville, Tennessee: Broadman Press, 1972); Waylon B. Moore, *New Testament Follow-up* (Grand Rapids, Michigan: Wm. B. Eerdmans, 1964).

PART THREE

The Process:
How to Build Multiplying Disciples

Spiritual Qualities of the Multiplying Disciplemaker

*"It is change, not
time, that turns
fools into wise
men and sinners
into saints"*
—A. W. Tozer

WE HAVE BEEN challenged by Edward Kimball's example in Part One to multiply ourselves spiritually through others to help accomplish the Great Commission of reaching the world for Christ.

In Part Two we have learned what a disciple is and why we should build disciples. We have studied some biblical examples of multiplication, and learned that the initial follow-up of a new convert is the actual starting point for disciple-making.

In the third part of this book we will focus initially on those spiritual qualities disciples need before they can multiply themselves, then in chapters eight through ten we will examine three basic principles of how to work with disciples so they will go on to multiply in future generations.

BE DOMINATED BY CHRIST'S GRACE

In 2 Timothy, chapter two, we find that the potential multiplier must first have a life that is dominated by Christ's grace. Paul commands Timothy to "be strong in the grace that is in Christ Jesus" (2 Timothy 2:1). This is the foundation for an effective ministry. "Not that we are sufficient of ourselves to think any thing as of ourselves; but our sufficiency is of God" (2 Corinthians 3:5). Truth that changes another life must come from the fountain of God's grace in our lives, which opens hearts and gives us a life-changing message to share.

Where does one get this grace? One source is mentioned in Hebrews 4:16: "Let us therefore come boldly unto the throne of grace, that we may obtain mercy, and find grace to help in time of need." As we come to God's throne in intercession he pours into our lives the very grace of Jesus Christ: we "obtain mercy" and "find grace." How needy we are—and how sufficient he is to supply all we lack to minister as we live in his presence.

Another power source for appropriating grace involves getting to know Christ experientially. "Grace and peace be multiplied unto you through the knowledge of God, and of Jesus our Lord" (2 Peter 1:2). Our knowledge of Christ increases as we take advantage of the means of grace—talking to him in prayer, and allowing him to speak to us through his word. Grace and peace result from spending time in both prayer and diligent study of the Scriptures.

Grace is also given to the humble (see 1 Peter 5:5-6). A person with a servant heart receives broad ministry opportunities. In addition as we minister humbly, our words become a source of grace (see Ephesians 4:29). Disobedience, however, can neutralize the operation of God's grace (see 2 Corinthians 6:1).

BE DEDICATED TO THE MINISTRY OF MULTIPLICATION

As disciples and potential multipliers we must also be committed to the ministry of multiplication as illustrated in 2 Timothy 2:2: "And the things that thou hast heard of me among many witnesses, the same commit thou to faithful men, who shall be able to teach others also." Timothy was to be a channel to others in sharing what Paul had taught him. Winning a person to Christ is the essential beginning, but only when that new believer in turn reaches another is there spiritual multiplication.

The word *commit* is imperative. We must commit to others what we have heard, seen, and experienced. For some, it is frightening to think of imparting their life experiences to a class or group, but we can begin by sharing with only one other person, and allow the hand of God to bless that relationship.

Paul specifically characterizes the men to whom we are to commit what we've learned: they are to be "faithful men," those who are in the word of God, for "faith cometh by hearing, and hearing by the word of God" (Romans 10:17). Select those who can be trusted.

Paul also stresses that they should be "able to teach others also." To be able to teach others, one must first be teachable. There are many in the church who are faithful in attendance and helping at special functions, but who do not pass on what they have heard and learned. Only God can put the desire to share the Scriptures within the heart of a person. Look for this kind of teachable individual. The potential in a man determines what you do with and through him.

In every church there are dozens of Christians who have never been challenged or shown how to transmit biblical truths to others effectively. The disciplemaker first learns how to do this; then he learns how to teach others to do it.

BE DISCIPLINED FOR A LIFE PLEASING TO GOD

The third quality which disciples need before they can multiply is discipline for a life that pleases God. We are on earth for his pleasure (see Revelation 4:11). Discipleship is not an easy, convenient routine; it is a demanding life. "Thou therefore endure hardness, as a good soldier of Jesus Christ. No man that warreth entangleth himself with the affairs of this life; that he may please him who hath chosen him to be a soldier" (2 Timothy 2:3-4). The multiplier is to expect hardness and to endure it. He is not to complain when his ministry becomes difficult.

Although we have freely volunteered, we have been chosen to be soldiers of Christ. A soldier is under orders, goal-oriented, and obedient to his supreme commander. We need discipline in order to live this kind of life.

The spiritual qualities which allow a disciple to become a multiplier, then, are first, a life dominated by Christ's grace, since his own powers and knowledge are insufficient; second, an unwavering dedication to the ministry of multiplication; and last, a disciplined life, since all of this is to be done to please God.

QUESTIONS FOR STUDY AND DISCUSSION

1. Describe the three qualities emphasized by Paul in 2 Timothy 2:1-4 as essentials for multiplying your ministry.

2. According to 2 Timothy 2:2, which link in the chain are you:
   a) A Barnabas who touched a Paul, starting the chain of multiplication
   b) One reached as a Timothy
   c) One of the "faithful men" being trained by a Timothy

    d) One of the "others also"
    e) Another?
    Explain your answer.

3. Discuss the "hardness" which must be endured as Christ's soldier (disciple). (See 2 Timothy 2:3-4.)

CHAPTER SEVEN

Have a Servant Heart

"You are meant to incarnate in your lives the theme of your adoration— you are to be taken, consecrated, broken and distributed, that you may be the means of grace and vehicles of the Eternal Charity"
—St. Augustine

A SERVANT HEART is one of God's supreme channels to win the lost to Christ. Building bridges of love into the hearts of those without Christ is preparation for sharing the gospel. Some people can be reached with a gospel presentation alone. Many others come to Christ only as we become their servants.

Do you know anyone whom you would classify as a servant of the Lord? Being a servant is an attitude, rather than a position. It involves a willingness to meet the needs of others at the servant's expense. Many times a servant will not be visible, but sooner or later others begin to depend on the servant and seek him out. Such a ministry of service can in time become the channel for modeling Christ to growing disciples.

THE MODEL SERVANT

Old Testament prophecy identifies the Messiah as the "suffering servant." Isaiah records, "Behold my servant, whom I uphold; mine elect, in whom my soul delighteth; I have put my spirit upon him: he shall bring forth judgment to the Gentiles" (Isaiah 42:1).

The personification of Jesus as a servant in this passage (verses one through four) and elsewhere is diametrically opposed to our fleshly desires to be served. However, our identity with Christ makes a servant heart necessary. Through service to the thankless, Jesus set a pattern for ministry that his disciples—and disciplemakers—must follow.

Before those who watched his every move, Christ spelled out the qualification for leadership: "And whosoever will be chief among you, let him be your servant: Even as the Son of man came not to be ministered unto, but to minister, and to give his life a ransom for many" (Matthew 20:27-28). The way up is down. Jesus came to minister, to serve as a slave.

When Abraham and his young nephew, Lot, had difficulty feeding their cattle in the same area, Abraham gave Lot first choice of all the land, although the privilege of first choice was Abraham's. Lot chose the land near Sodom. Then God spoke to Abraham and told him all the land was his. God made Abraham the undisputed master of all he could see after he chose to be a servant.

It may be difficult for Americans to understand the concept of servanthood. Our society and its emphasis on leisure has made service to others demeaning and belittling. To serve is to be at the bottom of the social ladder. Jesus counters all our pride with the divine viewpoint of John 12:24-25. In summary Christ says that to die to self is to live; to lose one's life is to find it. As we follow and serve Christ, not

58

self, we become available to serve others. Discipleship and service are irrevocably linked.

The example of our Lord throughout his life was to live always and only in complete submission to another. Jesus' deliberate choice in becoming God's servant to lost men is emphasized by Paul in Philippians 2:5-10, particularly verse seven: "But made himself of no reputation, and took upon him the form of a servant" (bond slave).

The nature of obedience as a slave is submission. The Father's will was Christ's will. The Father's word was his word. The Father's way was his way—by choice. This is submission. We must choose to live through the Spirit, always in complete submission to the Son.

As the outward manifestation of an obedient slave is submission, his inner manifestation as an obedient slave is meekness. What is meekness? The word *meek* means "tamed" or "broken," and thus controlled. Do you recall the only thing Jesus said to learn from him? "Learn of me; for I am meek and lowly in heart" (Matthew 11:29). Christ wants us to learn meekness from him.

Do you remember one thing Jesus said to copy as an example from his life? "If I then, your Lord and Master, have washed your feet; ye also ought to wash one another's feet. For I have given you an example, that ye should do as I have done to you" (John 13:14-15). Serving others is Christlike.

In 1 Peter 2:21-24 Peter reminds us of another example Jesus left for us:

> Because Christ also suffered for us, leaving us an example, that ye should follow his steps: . . . Who, when he was reviled, reviled not again; when he suffered, he threatened not; but committed himself to him that judgeth righteously.

The meekness of faith—suffering in silence—is the nature of

Christ. His disciples, then, should have the attribute of serving Christ and others by submission and meekness.

Jesus summarized his earthly pilgrimage in Luke 22:27: "For whether is greater, he that sitteth at meat, or he that serveth? . . . I am among you as he that serveth." Jesus broke bread at meals, replenished refreshments at Cana, and prepared a meal by the sea. He was constantly available any hour to broken bodies and hearts. Stripping to the loin cloth of a body slave, he washed the feet of his disciples and Judas.

Living with a Servant Heart

Paul began four letters by calling himself "the servant of Christ" (see Romans 1:1, Galatians 1:10, Philippians 1:1, and Titus 1:1). After three hard years at Ephesus, he remembers "serving the Lord with all humility of mind, and with many tears, . . . but none of these things move me, neither count I my life dear unto myself, . . . I am pure from the blood of all men. For I have not shunned to declare unto you all the counsel of God. . . . I have shewed you all things, how that so labouring ye ought to support the weak" (Acts 20:19-35).

Paul gave himself as the servant of Christ so that God could in turn give Paul to a city. Why did Paul face mobs and crowds who were unwilling to listen? Why did he accept beatings and jail at Philippi? As Christ's servant, Paul was led by the Spirit to remain silent about his Roman citizenship. He was thrown into the dungeon home of a jailer. Then God told his servant, Paul, to open his mouth and sing; only after this would he speak.

What an amazing thing for Paul to do, for God to do. Paul and Silas were willing to be jailed to be Christ's servants to that city and to bring a jailer and his family to Christ. The price of servanthood is high, but its rewards are priceless.

Sometimes I've prayed, "Lord give us this city for Christ." Yet God seems to be saying through Paul's ministry, "I will give you to the city."

Frequently—usually at suppertime—people knocked at our parsonage door wanting food, or money for auto repairs; one person even wanted an airplane ticket. What do you say to someone whose every fiber shows he's making his way through life by using his dirty children out in the old car to get things from people? We never turned down those needing food. Sometimes I couldn't stop giving a few dollars for gas, tires, spark plugs, transmission repairs, or another problem with a car.

But as the years went by, I became hardened. Home for an hour or two, seeing my family for the first time all day, I wanted to be left alone. Too soon I would be back out in my car visiting the lost until late that evening.

How lovingly the Lord persisted in seeking to teach me that food and money were not the real issues. My attitude was his target, but I failed so many times because behind my smile and my giving was anger at my church people down the block who directed the person to our door. I hated working my sixteen-hour days only to hand our groceries and money to those I sincerely felt didn't want to work.

My wife would say, "If you're going to help them, do it with a gracious spirit. You lose the credit from people if your attitude is sour, and you lose your reward from God." The Lord began to teach me "that the servant of the Lord must not strive; but be gentle unto all men" (2 Timothy 2:24). "And whatsoever you do, do it heartily, as unto the Lord, and not unto men; Knowing that of the Lord ye shall receive the reward of the inheritance: for ye serve the Lord Christ" (Colossians 3:23-24).

When I was serving myself, my attitude was wrong. But when I began to identify with Christ as his servant, opportunities became blessings, and sometimes I saw changes in the lives of others.

Scripture passages which emphasize the power of a servant heart to win the lost simply jump off the pages of the Bible.

> For though I be free from all men, yet have I made myself *servant* unto all, that I might gain the more. And unto the Jews I became as a Jew, . . . to them that are under the law, as under the law, that I might gain them, . . . to them that are without law, . . . to the weak . . . I am made all things to all men, that I might by *all means save some.* . . . and this I do for the gospel's sake (1 Corinthians 9:19-23, italics mine).

Paul made himself a servant; then he goes on to write that he was "made all things to all men." The Spirit began his work of making Paul available to be the servant of Christ. Then Paul became Christ's heart, hands, and feet of ministry to the doomed and dying.

But Paul is not finished. "Give none offence, neither to the Jews, nor to the Gentiles, nor to the church of God: Even as I please all men in all things, not seeking mine own profit, but the profit of many, that they may be saved" (1 Corinthians 10:32-33). Identification with Christ's life and message means a commitment to reach the lost through a servant heart. "Becoming all things to all men" is accomplished supernaturally. We must begin by yielding our rights, so that Christ may serve freely through us.

The Worlds We Evangelize

We are to evangelize the world where we live. The strata of our world are our home, neighborhood, community, school, job, and church. We become Christ's servants where we are now and as he leads "to the uttermost part of the earth."

In serving neighbors who were unsaved, we've picked up their garbage and trash when a can was overturned. The Lord led us to mow some yards. Through these and other experiences, the unsaved have become open to the gospel, and some have accepted Christ.

Getting this idea across to a person you're training involves doing specific projects together. Encourage your disciple toward creative projects involving his neighbors and friends, as well as the needy and elderly.

A disciple with a servant heart can express it in our busy world by:

- Being accessible (see Galatians 6:10)
- Being hospitable to all, and not a respecter of persons
- Giving value to people, thus making time to see them and to serve them
- Being creative in finding ways to help others (see Hebrews 10:24)
- Serving only when needed, rather than serving for recognition by others (see Galatians 1:10)
- Exercising his spiritual gift as one channel of service (see 1 Peter 4:10)

SERVING BROTHERS IN CHRIST

The names of those with a servant heart are like flakes of gold sprinkled throughout the last pages of some of Paul's letters. The family of Stephanas at Corinth was always reaching out in service to others. "Know the house of Stephanas; that it is the firstfruits of Achaia, and that they have *addicted* themselves to the ministry of the saints" (1 Corinthians 16:15, italics mine). *Addicted* literally means "appointed themselves." It refers to "a self-imposed duty."[1] In the same chapter Aquila and Priscilla have a church in their house in Corinth, as they did earlier in Rome. Epaphroditus' ministry of service to Paul is recorded to show us the value God places on everyday jobs (see Philippians 2:25-30).

One of the most exciting verses in Scripture for helping the disciple develop a servant heart is Hebrews 10:24: "And let us consider one another to provoke unto love and to good works." We are to contemplate others and stimulate them to love and ministry. We need to ask the Lord to put a person on our heart, to seek to understand their needs, then provoke them toward God.

A church family in whose lives we had an extended ministry stopped speaking to us. We sought to find the cause and apologize, but they wouldn't talk to us, or to others about the reason. Because of our genuine love and respect, we prayed daily for them. Nothing seemed to happen. Then the Lord showed me the need to apply Hebrews 10:24. My wife and I decided together, after prayer, to show our love by sending the family flowers. Lovely mums were ordered, but two weeks went by without a noticeable change of attitude by our friends. We checked with the florist—the delivery had been made. So we prayed. A week later the couple came into the office and we talked. They shared the problem and said they would join another church if I felt that was best. I told them I loved them, prayed for them, and needed their ministry. God joined hearts together again that afternoon, and our relationship was healed. Hebrews 10:24 is a verse I encourage disciples to learn and apply.

A large group of English pastors came to one of D. L. Moody's great Northfield Bible Conferences in the late 1800s. As the custom was in England, each pastor put his shoes outside his room to be cleaned by the hall servants overnight.

However, there were no hall servants at that meeting.

Moody was walking through the dormitory that evening and saw a dozen or more dirty pairs of shoes in the halls. Seeing this as an opportunity to serve his brothers, Moody mentioned the shoes to some of the ministerial students. There was only silence. Moody returned to the dormitory and gathered up all the shoes. He carefully marked the room numbers on the shoes so there would be no mix-up. Alone in his room, Moody began to clean and polish the shoes. A friend knocked on Moody's door and found him violently attacking the pile of shoes.

When the English ministers opened their doors the next morning, their shoes were shined, but they were none the wiser. Moody didn't tell anyone, but his tired friend told a few people. During the rest of the conference, different men volunteered to secretly shine the shoes.

A servant heart is catching! What we catch of Christ can then be caught by those we would mold into the image of our Servant Lord. A servant heart will attract others to you, make them comfortable with you, and eventually make the disciples you're training want to be more like Jesus. "For God is not unrighteous to forget your work and labour of love, which ye have shewed toward his name, in that ye have ministered to the saints, and do minister" (Hebrews 6:10).

NOTES

1. Archibald Robinson and Alfred Plummer, *International Critical Commentary: A Critical and Exegitical Commentary on the First Epistle of St. Paul to the Corinthians* (New York: Charles Scribner's Sons, 1911), page 395.

QUESTIONS FOR STUDY AND DISCUSSION

1. Why is biblical leadership linked to servanthood? How does this concept compare with your experiences at work, in the church, and elsewhere?

2. How can we learn meekness from Christ, thus fulfilling his command (see Matthew 11:28-30)?

3. Can you recall some of the personal costs to you in being Christ's servant to people?

4. Read aloud Hebrews 10:24.
   a) List a person in your church who needs to be provoked to love. Pray, asking God what you might do to stimulate this person toward good works. Try baking a cake, sending flowers, or writing a thank-you note. For a special impact, don't sign your name; deliver the gift secretly.
   b) List as many as three people without Christ in each of the worlds of your witness (see pages 62 and 63). Pray daily for them. Ask God what he would have you do to apply Hebrews 10:24 someway to their lives. God will single out a person in each strata for you to serve. Share the results with other disciples.

CHAPTER EIGHT

Presence with the Disciple

*"Availability
is rarer
than ability"*
—anonymous

ACTS 20:17-38 DESCRIBES Paul's years at Ephesus, a fellowship which emerged from idolatry into a full-grown church with well established shepherd leaders in just three years. Paul built this church by using three principles for building spiritual multipliers.

The first principle is the need for extended *presence* with your disciples. The second is the dimension of caring and love associated with a *parent heart* (chapter nine). Third, Paul used the principle of *pacesetting* (chapter ten).

WITH HIM: THE PRINCIPLE OF PRESENCE

Jesus chose the twelve disciples to be with him to share his life, as well as to observe and learn from his ministry by watching and copying him. In Mark 3:14 we read that "he ordained twelve, that they should be with him, and that he might send them forth to preach." This verse contains three steps in the process of building multipliers: selecting them, training them, and sending them forth. Each of these steps included Christ's presence.

Thus, one critical issue in any biblical discipling ministry is time, for investing one's life in a growing disciple cannot be done without spending extended time with him. The size of Christ's team of men was related to his commitment to make his time available to them. He was not able to give his time to everyone. After healing the demoniac, for instance, he told him to return home.

The number of people you can invest your life in is limited by the time you are willing to commit to meeting their individual needs. An hour a week with a group can be simply academic. It will not necessarily produce quality disciples because it is not modeled on Christ's example of investing time—that is, himself—in the lives of others. Intercession for those we disciple is the unseen inner core of love; spending time together is the public expression of a disciplemaking lifestyle.

Throughout the Acts and the Epistles we see the extraordinary amount of time Paul spent in group fellowship and training. Paul was with the new believers "at all seasons" (Acts 20:18). He summarizes his time at Ephesus by writing, "Remember that for three years I never stopped warning each of you night and day with tears" (Acts 20:31, NIV).

What did Paul do during his three years at Ephesus? In addition to supporting himself and his team, he was also preaching and teaching "publicly and from house to house" (Acts 20:20). He also showed the believers all of the principles that are essential to serving and evangelizing in a pagan capital (see Acts 20:35). Paul's review of his ministry to the Ephesian elders reminds us of the absolute priority he gave to building a church fellowship of multiplying believers.

Leadership training was built into the fabric of evangelism and teaching, so that Paul left elders who could minister independently of his presence. Because Christ's love was poured out through Paul and his team, it is no wonder that as he left Ephesus, "they all wept sore, and fell on Paul's neck, and kissed him" (Acts 20:37).

Many pastorates have become short-term assignments. Missionary ministries are increasingly facing time limits as governments change and doors close to many foreigners. As cautioned in Stephen Neill's piercing words, "The missionary [or pastor] . . . must consciously guard himself against the illusion of permanence in which so many of his predecessors have become trapped."[1] The Christian worker will not become discouraged, however small his group, if he can focus on individual disciples. The lasting impact of his ministry will rest on those trained disciples he leaves behind!

The quality of training in disciplemaking must be extremely high, or the mutations in the third and fourth generations will not resemble biblically-defined disciples. The further downstream from the source one drinks, the more polluted the water. Our life is our message. Abraham Lincoln said, "I don't know who my grandfather was. I am much more concerned to know what his grandson will be."[2]

WHAT DO YOU TEACH A HUNGRY DISCIPLE?

If a person said to you, "I'll give you ten hours a week for the next six months: feed me, teach me; I'm available," what would you do? Many in the church would have difficulty answering this question.

69

First, here is what *not* to do.

- Shoot the breeze. You have specific biblical goals to achieve. Don't waste time on nonessentials.
- Gripe about the church.
- Cry on each other's shoulder.
- Go through Bible study material in a lecturer/listener format.

Certain biblical essentials comprise the heart of the principle of presence. Five priorities are involved when we meet with disciples regularly, and the amount of time spent on each one varies from meeting to meeting, as the Holy Spirit leads.

Progress. Telling isn't teaching; and listening isn't learning. Share progress made. Insist on checking up on the previous assignment. Jesus was never easy on anything that would neutralize reaching future generations. A check-up guarantees you will have no freeloaders who are not giving priority to study.

Biblical principles. Discuss biblical principles with the disciple. Teach doctrine and how to apply God's word to daily life.

A suggested list of Bible-related subjects to cover over a period of several months includes the following topics (most of them are covered in my *Building Disciples Notebook*[3]).

- Assurance of salvation
- The quiet time
- Prayer
- The Holy Spirit
- Confessing sin
- Victory over sin
- Separation from the world, the flesh, and the Devil

- Fellowship (in and out of church)
- The Bible: hearing, reading, memorizing, meditating, and study methods
- Claiming the promises of God
- Applying the word to life
- Witnessing: how to give a personal testimony and a basic presentation of the gospel
- Lordship of Christ
- Personal relationships: the unsaved, family, church, man-woman
- World vision and missions
- Goal-setting
- Finances
- Use of time
- Follow-up and discipling
- How to develop a man-to-man ministry
- Will of God (how to be guided by the Spirit)
- Control of the tongue
- Attitudes
- Second coming of Christ
- Satan

Though no two disciplers would agree on the order of these training priorities, most would generally agree on the content. Individuals differ so widely that the presentation of these subjects and their applications will need to be adjusted for the needs of each person.

Personal lessons taught to you by the Spirit of Christ should be shared. Nothing lifts a relationship to a biblical plane more quickly than showing a disciple a scriptural principle which has been put into effect in your life.

Handling problems. Seek to solve current difficulties and prevent future problems which retard growth in the disciple's personal life. As the relationship becomes more open and free, the disciple will begin to share where he is hurting, questioning, doubting, and having difficulties.

Most of the New Testament letters were written to meet problems in the local church. A high percentage of their content deals with problems of doctrine, conduct, and interpersonal relationships. Many of us learn and grow in the context of confronting and solving problems. The Christian life includes suffering and learning to handle pressure (see Philippians 1:29, 3:10; 1 Peter 2:20-21).

Carefully monitor the amount of time you give to problem-solving, however, for there must be balance. Some people seem to live just to vent their problems, and they are easily recognized. They generally want to share not only with you, but with others as well. They shop for counselors who will agree with them.

Prayer. Pray together in intercession and praise. One of the most intimate activities in life is praying with another person. You will not get to know another person well until you have prayed with him a great deal. Nothing helps you learn where another is hurting, or what their needs, desires, and goals are faster than protracted times of prayer.

Use prayer lists. Encourage your disciple to keep prayer pages where he records specific requests, answers, Scriptures claimed, and dates which chronicle the faithfulness of God in answering his prayers. Reviewing those pages will feed his faith for further prayer as he sees the miraculous ways God has dealt with him in the past.

Practice. The first four essentials of progress, principles, problems, and prayer must be linked with putting it all into practice. Channeling your time together toward ministering to other people's needs will provide fresh and practical scriptural applications. Do things together, especially sharing Christ with the lost. This is how you demonstrate becoming a doer of the word, not just a hearer (see James 1:22). Your intercession for him and your witnessing with him binds you together in mutual spiritual growth.

QUESTIONS FOR STUDY AND DISCUSSION

1. Share some examples from your own life of occasions when another Christian spent an hour or so alone with you in a way that built you up spiritually.

2. Discuss how you have learned through the teaching ministry of another person in school, at home, at work, or during times of recreation.

3. Discuss the time factor in learning to do anything. How much time is needed to learn to tie a shoelace, sing a song well, teach a class of adults, witness to a lost person, or counsel another individual with a problem?

4. How should discipling time differ from other structured class and fellowship times?

5. Give a time value to the five "Ps" in this chapter when meeting with another person for discipling. Why is time a major factor in many areas of discipling?

6. Review the topics that may be shared with another person. Which seem most important, less important, or unnecessary? Are there some topics you would add, or changes you would make in the suggested order? Explain your approach.

7. What is the difference between telling, teaching, and training? Why is training essential in discipling?

═══════════════ NOTES ═══════════════

1. Stephen Neill, as quoted by Ted Engstrom, *What in the World Is God Doing?* (Waco, Texas: Word Books Inc., 1978), page 61.

2. Abraham Lincoln, as quoted in "Quotable Quotes," *Reader's Digest*, December, 1979, page 157.

3. Waylon B. Moore, *Building Disciples Notebook* (available from Missions Unlimited Inc., Box 8203, Tampa, Florida 33603). The notebook includes studies and devotional aids for a period of from twenty-six weeks to three years.

CHAPTER NINE

Have a Parent Heart

*"Be parent,
not possessor.
Be attendant,
not master"*
—Lao Tzu

THERE ARE MANY spiritual babes in our churches, but there are few spiritual parents assuming responsibility for them.

Paul said he was confident that God would mature those he had saved (see Philippians 1:6). What was the reason for his confidence? As a spiritual parent, he always prayed for his babes in Christ (see Philippians 1:3-4), and he loved them, saying, "It is right for me to feel this way about all of you, since *I have you in my heart*" (Philippians 1:7, NIV, italics mine).

Those who want to multiply themselves throughout the world must be lovingly responsible for another's life, just as a parent is with a child. Paul ministered both as a mother *and* as a father to the new Christians at Thessalonica (see 1 Thessalonians 2:7 and 11). The only way a father or mother can train is person-to-person. A three-year-old has different needs than a ten-year-old. Similarly, the spiritual needs in the church can best be met by individual care and training.

It is not easy being a disciplemaking parent. There is a personal price to pay in love and discipline in working with a soul that will live for eternity. Once such an assignment from Christ is accepted, a parent-child discipling relationship sometimes continues for a lifetime, growing into a mature colaboring fellowship.

To reach into another's life and make a lasting deposit of the grace of God is such a great privilege that the whole church should be running toward such an opportunity! For once a spiritual investment is made in another's life, you share in all the glory of the eternal rewards reaped through that life forever. Paul referred to this when he wrote to the growing Christians he had trained, saying, "For ye are our glory and joy" (1 Thessalonians 2:20).

We have a four-fold responsibility as spiritual parents to love, feed, protect, and train our disciples.

A PARENT LOVES HIS SPIRITUAL CHILDREN

"By this shall all men know that ye are my disciples, if ye have love one to another" (John 13:35). The overriding motivation throughout Christ's ministry to his disciples was love; and it should be the most recognizable character trait of each of us as twentieth century disciples.

Jesus did not always approve of his disciples' attitudes or desires, but he always accepted and loved them as individuals. In his presence the disciples felt freedom and comfort. They *knew* he was different. When Christ's enemies said he was a friend of publicans and sinners, they unwittingly drew attention to his love for others.

Love is an attitude which is committed to meeting the

deepest needs in another person, no matter what the cost. Paul told the elders at Ephesus, "I kept back nothing that was profitable unto you, but have shewed you, and have taught you" (Acts 20:20). He reminded the Thessalonians, "We were willing to have imparted unto you . . . our own souls, because ye were dear unto us" (1 Thessalonians 2:8). Just as Christ gave himself in love for us, our love must express itself in giving up ourselves and our rights to help others.

This loving commitment to others' needs often requires facing problems head-on. Paul reminded the Ephesians about a tough problem in their midst: "I ceased not to warn every one night and day with tears" (Acts 20:31). What bold love it took for Paul to warn constantly and caringly until the issue was faced and conquered.

It has not always been so with me, nor may it be so with you. I have sometimes avoided a loving, private confrontation. I have been fearful and hesitant to love some people enough to face them with their sin and humbly seek to lead them to repentance and restitution. But that is not as it should be. "Hereby perceive we the love of God, because he laid down his life for us: and we ought to lay down our lives for the brethren" (1 John 3:16).

"Laying down our lives" means reckoning ourselves dead to sin and alive to Christ daily so that we become his living channels of love (see John 17:26). Love is the test of the Spirit's control of our lives (see Galatians 5:22) and results in a closeness with others that makes multiplication through them more certain. This love for our disciples means, however, "not making converts to our ways of thinking, but making disciples of Jesus."[1]

Years ago I shared with a deacon of my church that he had the gift of shepherding and should seriously consider entering the pastorate. During this time some unpleasant things happened, and he left the church. People questioned me about him. I steadfastly refused to say anything negative about him, and continued to believe he could serve Christ in a broader ministry. I was also fervently praying for him.

As the years passed, he did answer God's call to a full-time pastorate, and is now having a dynamic ministry. Recently, we met for the first time in years. He said, "Much of what I use that works and that has changed my life came under your ministry, Pastor." There is never a loss when we love!

The true love of Paul for his spiritual children shines from the pages of 2 Corinthians. Despite being misunderstood and falsely accused, Paul carried on. At one point, with his heart bursting with love for the Corinthians, he exclaimed, "And I will very gladly spend and be spent for you; though the more abundantly I love you, the less I be loved" (2 Corinthians 12:15).

The power to love is never dependent on people or things; it comes from a relationship with the Holy Spirit (see Romans 5:5). His fruit is love (see Galatians 5:22). Lack of love reveals a lack of an intimate relationship with the Holy Spirit. If you allow the Spirit to empower you to love others, your love will be returned in your discipling relationships. You will achieve your goals through love.

A PARENT FEEDS HIS SPIRITUAL CHILDREN

In summarizing his three years at Ephesus in Acts 20, Paul recalls his constant feeding of the word of God to the disciples: "I kept back nothing that was profitable unto you . . . and have taught you" (Acts 20:20); "I have not shunned to declare unto you all the counsel of God" (Acts 20:27).

At first, an infant is fed by others; he then advances to feeding himself as a child, and finally moves on to feeding others as an adult. One of the disciplemaker's primary goals is to teach a disciple how to feed himself so he can eventually feed others also. Here are some of the ways you can help him get the word of God into his life.

Feed Him by Teaching the Quiet Time
Daniel 6:10-11 is an effective model of a quiet time with God, for it lists *where* Daniel prayed, *when* he prayed, and *what* he prayed for.

A definite place. We need a regular place to be alone with the Lord, free from distractions. If your home isn't quiet, perhaps somewhere outside will work better for you: in your car, parked on a quiet street; walking in the early morning in the neighborhood; or even jogging alone. But wherever you choose, be sure you enter your closet, the place of private devotion, daily (see Matthew 6:6).

A definite time. Meeting God in the morning was the habit of Christ (see Mark 1:35). This is the best time for many, because it is a good preparation for the busy day ahead. For victory in getting up to meet with the Lord, make an appointment with him the night before. Ten minutes of fellowship with God in the morning is better than none at all; better to begin with a short time and let it grow naturally. Your time will lengthen as you hunger to know him better and experience him in your life.

A definite content. A quiet time is a feeding time for the Christian. You fill your mind and spirit with the presence of God, feeding on his word as he talks to you. Then you converse with him in prayer.

Prepare the night before. Have your Bible, devotional materials, and notebook ready. The Bible and devotional literature are your food. Use the notebook to record new thoughts and prayer requests. Also write down answers to prayer you have received.

Feed Him by Teaching How to Take Sermon Notes
We forget about 90 percent of what we hear. Taking sermon notes cuts that percentage of loss by at least half. One quick way to teach a disciple how to feed himself is by helping him learn how to take notes on each message from the pulpit.

Sermon notes should be of uniform size each week. They should include the name of the speaker, date, sermon title, Bible passage, cross-references, an outline of the content, and any specific sentences. The notes can be filed by Bible book or by subject matter. They are then available for meditation, for study, or for use in preparing one's own devotional talks.

Teach your spiritual child to discover the main lesson of the sermon, then how to apply the basic truths to his life situations. The members of the congregation are as responsible to leave with the sermon as the preacher is to prepare it. And both are accountable to God to live it!

Feed Him by Teaching How to Read the Bible
We remember only a little more of what we read (60 to 80 percent) than what we hear, so again it is imperative to take notes to improve our retention. As the disciple reads, here are some specific things he can look for and jot down notes on in the text:

- The main lesson
- What the passage teaches about God the Father, the Son, and the Holy Spirit
- A verse which summarizes the passage
- A command to obey
- What God is teaching right now from this passage

It is important for the disciple to read through the entire Bible to grasp its unity. Reading specific books in one sitting is especially valuable in meeting individual needs. Assign regular readings, with the goal that Bible reading become a lifelong habit. Help your disciple by encouraging him and checking up to see how he is profiting from his reading.

Feed Him by Teaching Bible Study Methods
Learning how to study the Bible for himself will set the disciple free, enabling him to "eat of the word" whenever he wishes instead of being dependent upon someone else for his essential spiritual food. When teaching study methods, expect the disciple to spend a minimum of twenty minutes daily on his homework.

Four methods of study, in particular, result in dynamic growth. They are *verse meditation*, in which one verse is studied in depth; *chapter analysis*, in which one book is studied chapter by chapter; *word studies*, in which specific words like *joy, love,* and *peace* are studied; and *character studies*, in which the people of the Bible are analyzed. The richness of these four kinds of personal, self-feeding study prepares the layman to find God's will throughout his lifetime.

Here are some tips for my favorite Bible study plan, the chapter analysis approach. This requires only a Bible, paper, and pen. Suggest to the disciple at least four things:

Paraphrase. Using your own words, write out what the chapter reveals. This helps you understand it fully and makes the chapter your own.

Questions. Write down anything about the text which you do not understand. Also, list questions you think others may have, but which you have found answers to. This helps when you begin to teach others. Give a Scripture reference as a basis for answering questions whenever possible.

Cross-references. Find a cross-reference (another verse which contains a similar or related truth in another portion of Scripture) for each verse in the chapter. Thus, the Bible becomes its own best commentary, explaining and illuminating each passage studied.

Application. Prayerfully write down a personal application based on a verse in the chapter. Explain what you are going to do, in God's strength, to apply this passage in your daily life. Be specific: for example, instead of writing, "I'm going to pray more next week," which is much too general, write, "I have the sin of prayerlessness. Next week I will pray for at least ten minutes daily." Check up on yourself to make sure you carry out your application. Faithfully applying God's word will help you to become a doer, not just a hearer of the word.

Psalm 1, Psalm 23, and the short New Testament books such as Philemon, Philippians, and 1 Thessalonians are excellent portions for a disciple who is beginning to learn how to study the Bible. One or two weeks is usually a good time frame for each chapter.

When you've taught your disciple how to study the Bible, be sure to teach him how to teach others. In all of your discipling, keep in mind the ultimate goal of multiplying disciplemakers—those who are trained and skilled in transmitting what they have learned.

Feed Him by Teaching Scripture Memory

Memorizing Scripture results in many blessings and greater power. A disciple can defeat temptation and walk in victory over any sin (see Psalm 119:11). He can live a successful and fruitful life (see Psalm 1:2-3). He will discover new interest in the Bible and greater understanding. His ability to teach will improve (see Colossians 3:16). He will experience a new power to witness, and see positive results (see 1 Peter 3:15). He will know more of God's will for his life as more light shines along the path (see Psalm 119:105). He can experience greater growth in his faith, new joy, and a more positive spirit in his daily life (see Psalm 119:103). He can pray with new assurance. Learning Bible promises increases boldness in prayer (see John 15:7).

All these blessings and more will result when a disciple memorizes Scripture and couples it with meditation for application.

How to memorize a verse. Your attitude makes the difference. In learning verses, you have the help of the Holy Spirit to "guide you into all truth." You "*can do all things through Christ, which strengthens you*" (Philippians 4:13, italics mine). He will empower you to learn if you ask him to.

1. After you have selected a verse, read it in context in the Bible. Reading the chapter that includes the verse will help you understand it. Read the verse thoughtfully several times aloud. If it has not been done for you, decide what the topic of the verse is.[2]

2. Learn the verse in this order: the topic, verse reference, first phrase, and verse reference again. Repeat that much several times. Then start over; always begin with the reference, add another phrase, and end with the reference. Continue "bite by bite" until you have learned the whole verse.

3. Review the verse during the day; use spare moments. Say it at meals, when traveling or waiting, and before you sleep. Ask someone to check your memorization. Repeat the verse daily for several weeks. Review it weekly thereafter.

4. Begin by memorizing two verses a week.

5. Meditate on each verse you learn. Pray it back to God. Ask him for an experience with the verse in your life. Each verse contains something for you to know, to stop, to begin, or to share. The ultimate purpose through each verse is to identify with Christ in his will, to know him better, and to multiply his glory.

A PARENT PROTECTS HIS SPIRITUAL CHILDREN

Satan has planned the systematic destruction of Christ's disciples through bitterness, discouragement, impatience, and other sins. Though the tragedies are legion, the power to withstand Satan's onslaughts is instantly available as we appropriate the very life of Christ. "Greater is he that is in you, than he that is in the world" (1 John 4:4).

Christ set the example for us as protective spiritual parents when he said to Peter, "Behold, Satan hath desired to have you, that he may sift you as wheat: but I have prayed for thee, that thy faith fail not: and when thou art converted, strengthen thy brethren" (Luke 22:31-32).

Protection from Temptation
Three basic temptations which Satan uses to draw us into sin are found in 1 John 2:15-16.

> Love not the world, neither the things that are in the world. If any man love the world, the love of the Father is not in him. For all that is in the world, the lust of the flesh, and the lust of the eyes, and the pride of life, is not of the Father, but is of the world.

The lust of the flesh. Lust begins with a *look*. "Let thine eyes look right on, and let thine eyelids look straight before thee. Ponder the path of thy feet, and let all thy ways be established. Turn not to the right hand nor to the left: remove thy foot from evil" (Proverbs 4:25-27).

Helping disciples means observing their conduct with the opposite sex. Honest and frank words on this subject, spoken in love, must be shared with both single and married disciples so they learn how to "keep thy heart with all diligence; for out of it are the issues of life" (Proverbs 4:23).

The lust of the eyes. The desire for money and the desire for possessions are equally destructive to disciples. Both are a result of an ungodly concentration on the cares of this world.

Money in itself is not evil; rightly used, it can be a means for effective ministry to a greater number of people. However, the love of it is evil.

> But they that will be rich fall into temptation and a snare, and into many foolish and hurtful lusts, which drown men in destruction and perdition. For the love of money is the root of all evil: which while some coveted after, they have erred from the faith, and pierced themselves through with many sorrows (1 Timothy 6:9-10).

"You cannot serve both God and money" (Matthew 6:24, NIV).

The key is not being possessed by money. Ascertain whether your disciple has money under control or if money has him under control. Watch his motivation in business. Observe how much energy he devotes to obtaining money. What are his priorities? Does he have time for the Lord, his family, and his church ministry? Observe how he spends and saves. What does he talk about? Share sound principles on handling finances to help your disciple stay out of debt, for this will give him mobility and free him to answer God's call.

Closely related to the desire for money is the desire for possessions. We should ask ourselves, How much do we really need for basic living? "And having food and raiment let us be therewith content" (1 Timothy 6:8). Everything else is extra: houses, cars, and educational diplomas. Thank God for the extras, but don't set your heart on them.

Some missionaries had to leave Vietnam with less than two hours notice. They have something to share about "the loss of all things" (Philippians 3:8). What little they brought out with them revealed their sense of values. Some brought out family pictures or another portable sentimental object, but not much else.

These missionaries can testify from experience that we are not to lay up for ourselves treasures "where moth and rust doth corrupt, and where thieves break through and steal: But lay up for yourselves treasures in heaven" (Matthew 6:19-20).

Think through all of your possessions. What do you truly need? What can you do without? Now, mentally surrender to God the right to have *any* of these things. When you do that, the things will lose their hold on you and you will use them with the awareness that they are God's, not yours.

The pride of life. The temptation to be proud often manifests itself in an excessive desire for self-recognition. When Satan can't stop a man with impurity or trap him in the money web, he whispers, "You need more appreciation. You've done a good job and no one understands." Many soldiers have lost the battle of multiplying disciples because "they loved the praise of men more than the praise of God" (John 12:43). Watch out for injured pride, sourness, sulking, and bitterness in your disciples. Much of this has its roots in the desire for personal glory.

The desire to be appreciated and honored is natural; however, it is a luxury few can afford. "Say little, serve all, pass on," is a devastating motto to human pride. Remember, the Lord is the rewarder of them that diligently seek him. He, himself, is our ultimate reward (see Genesis 15:1).

The pride of life can also take the form of excessive competition. We want to be the best we can before the Lord, so that we will please him in everything we do. While healthy competition can promote a desire for excellence, too much concentration on self can cloud our vision of the needs of others. We need to keep in mind Paul's words to the Philippians: "Let nothing be done through strife or vainglory; but in lowliness of mind let each esteem others better than themselves. Look not every man on his own things, but every man also on the things of others" (Philippians 2:3-4).

Protection Through Discipline
When God's warnings are unheeded and the disciple sins, the spiritual parent must discipline. This is an essential ministry in the church. "But *exhort one another daily,* while it is called Today; lest any of you be hardened through the deceitfulness of sin" (Hebrews 3:13, italics mine).

The master passage on discipline is Hebrews 12:5-13. We are to *discipline* those in our charge; *we are not to punish!* The goal of punishment is the stopping of a habit or offense, but discipline's aim is the restoration of fellowship with God.

To be honest and open with others about their sins is a delicate but essential matter. Not only is rebuke and exhortation a fast way to recovery and spiritual growth, but it also demonstrates a rare love by the rebuker: few are willing to risk losing a relationship in order to discipline.

Paul uses a number of words to describe loving confrontation: *charge, admonish, rebuke, reprove, correct, exhort,* and even *comfort.* If a spiritual parent allows a disciple to keep disobeying the word without rebuking him lovingly, he is failing to exercise genuine love in the relationship.

Discipline in love is essential *now* if disciples are later to grow up loving purity and seeking to live a godly life. Little seeds of sin produce large trees which block the sunlight of God's purposes. A failure to correct and discipline our natural children while they are young means those "little" shortcomings eventually will grow into big problems. The same is true in our relationships with our spiritual children. Correct disobedience quickly. "Because sentence against an evil work is not executed speedily, therefore the heart of the sons of men is fully set in them to do evil" (Ecclesiastes 8:11).

Years later those who have been lovingly rebuked will look back with joy that God loved them enough to touch their lives permanently through one who cared enough to discipline. "He that rebuketh a man *afterwards* shall find more favour than he that flattereth with the tongue" (Proverbs 28:23, italics mine).

How to admonish in love. When sharing with disciples about sin in their lives, do so in the light of 1 Corinthians 13 and Galatians 6:1-3. As the Spirit leads you to confront the disciple, here are some ground rules for sharing.

1. The word of God is always the basis for admonition. It is imperative that we know that the offense is clearly contrary to Scripture (see Titus 2:1).

2. Use discretion. Timing is essential. Sometimes it is God's plan for us to apply this truth: "The discretion of a man deferreth his anger; and it is his glory to pass over a transgression" (Proverbs 19:11).

3. The discipler must fulfill the requirement of Galatians 6:1; "ye which are spiritual." We must be controlled by the Holy Spirit. We must have victory in our own hearts over the area of guilt revealed in the other's life.

4. We are not called to confront everyone we meet who has a sin problem. Winning the heart is a key to a positive response, but it takes time. Also, we are not everyone's spiritual parents.

5. The admonition must be reasonable, given in a loving manner, as from a brother, and it should convey compassion and tenderness (see 2 Corinthians 2:4).

6. Admonishing another must be done in meekness (see Galatians 6:1). Remember, this same thing could happen to you someday—or may already have. Speak carefully, and with a humble heart.

7. Do it privately (see Proverbs 25:9 and Matthew 18:15).

8. Do it with perseverance. Don't allow yourself to get

weary and discouraged. Keep at it but don't nag. Be finished with it afterwards (see Proverbs 13:19 and 28:23).

A PARENT TRAINS HIS SPIRITUAL CHILDREN

The responsibility of the spiritual parent to train his child captures the basic intent of this book. Review all the training chapters and prepare for yourself a basic training plan for your disciple, not something which is inflexible, but something which does contain the essentials of discipleship. When to give those essentials and how to teach them will differ with individuals, but all of the basics should be included in each individual's training.

QUESTIONS FOR STUDY AND DISCUSSION

1. Why is the comparison between physical and spiritual parents so widely used in Scripture? What can we learn from it? (See 1 Corinthians 4:15-16; 2 Corinthians 12:14-15; Galatians 4:19; 2 Timothy 1:2; Titus 1:4; 3 John 4.)

2. Which of the spiritual parent's four responsibilities toward those he is helping is the most used, and which is the least used in your
   a) Sunday school class
   b) Worship service
   c) Church training
   d) Personal training from someone else?

3. What could be done now within your fellowship to stimulate a loving response toward each new church member or new believer?

4. Discuss anything from your quiet time this week that you've found helpful.

5. How can you encourage another in his daily time with God?

6. Discuss the possibility of
   a) taking sermon notes and sharing them as a family.
   b) doing a chapter analysis Bible study together on Psalm 1 and Psalm 23.

7. Discuss the three areas of temptation that can destroy growing disciples. How can you help someone you know experience victory in one of those areas?

———————————— NOTES ————————————

1. Oswald Chambers, *So Send I You* (Fort Washington, Pennsylvania: Christian Literature Crusade, 1972), page 75.

2. The *Topical Memory System*, published by The Navigators (Colorado Springs, Colorado: NavPress, 1969), is available in several translations, and sold at Christian bookstores.

CHAPTER TEN

Be a Pacesetter

*"One living
sermon is worth
one hundred
explanations"*
—Robert Coleman

PACESETTING IS A term borrowed from running. One runner leads the way, setting a pace for the others to follow. That way they won't go too fast, and burn themselves out, or too slowly, and not finish well. If the disciple has no pace set for him, it is very difficult for him to know how he is doing.

JESUS SET OUR EXAMPLE

Jesus taught first by the example of his daily life, which he shared openly with his disciples. J. M. Price writes, "The first and probably the greatest aspect of their training was personal association with him and learning through example and imitation. They saw him as he sympathized, comforted, fed, and healed, and caught his spirit."[1]

Jesus relied a great deal on teaching by example. He commanded his disciples to testify of him because, as he told them, "Ye have been *with me* from the beginning" (John 15:27, italics mine). Later, when the members of the Sanhedrin observed the boldness of Peter and John, "they took knowledge of them, that they had been with Jesus" (Acts 4:13). Time spent watching and learning from the example of Jesus was evident publicly in the lives of Peter and John.

PAUL—ANOTHER PACESETTER

Paul also set a deliberate example for his followers. He commanded them, "Those things, which ye have both learned, and received, and heard, and seen in me, do: and the God of peace shall be with you" (Philippians 4:9). "Yourselves know how ye ought to follow us: . . . to make ourselves an ensample unto you to follow us" (2 Thessalonians 3:7-9).

Paul's example as a pacesetter paved the way for his disciples to become multipliers. In 1 Thessalonians 1:6-9 we learn that the new believers (the second generation) were followers of Paul (the first generation), so they immediately reached out in evangelism. In verse seven Paul refers to the Thessalonians as examples to others (who would become a third spiritual generation). The Greek word for *example* also means "mold" or "pattern." The first imitators of Paul had now become the molds through which others could, in turn, become imitators; thus multiplication was occurring.

SPIRITUAL QUALITIES OF THE PACESETTER

What makes a person want to follow another in a genuine,

biblical way? There must be in the pacesetter's life certain qualities worth copying that challenge the disciple. You must exemplify these qualities if you are going to multiply yourself through others.

Surrender. There must be both an initial surrender (see Romans 12:1) and a daily renewal as Christ continually reveals new truth through the word. Such surrender means giving up rights; not only my individual rights, but my job, family, and future must all be committed to Christ.

Oswald Chambers remarks on the refusal to surrender: "If I hear the call of God and refuse to obey, I become the dullest, most commonplace of Christians because I have seen and heard and refused to obey."[2] If you are finding anything dull about the Christian life, perhaps there is an area of unconfessed disobedience. Ask yourself, Is Christ the Lord, right now, this moment, in every area of my life? The answer must be yes before you can lead others.

Separation. There must be separation from worldly things and a worldly sense of values. We are to have a cutting edge of purity which transforms people without a vision into goal-oriented disciples. We must ask ourselves, Is my life Christlike? Will it glorify him? Are we listening to the "still small voice" of God? Do we recognize that our citizenship, goals, and future are in heaven (see Colossians 3:1)?

Peter wrote, "Wherefore, beloved, seeing that ye look for such things, be diligent that ye may be found of him in peace, without spot, and blameless" (2 Peter 3:14). He urged the believers in his day to cultivate an awareness of the second coming of Christ in order to separate themselves from worldly concerns.

Basically, worldliness is the exclusion of the lordship of Christ at the center of one's life. It is a mental attitude of wanting to do things your own way. The acrostic TIME is a good, positive test of the will of God:

Time. Is it my servant or my master?
Integrity. What am I becoming by this act? Is this something that will help me grow spiritually?
Ministry. Am I able to minister to another's deepest needs through this action?
Evangelism. Does this choice enable me to advance the Great Commission?

Systematic discipline. Another important quality which characterizes an effective multiplier is systematic discipline in the word and prayer—the basics of the spiritual life.

You will lead others if you have disciplined growth habits. As those who follow you adapt your habits, they, too, will grow.

LEADERSHIP QUALITIES OF THE PACESETTER

In addition to the spiritual qualities, here are some basics in leadership which every builder of multipliers needs to have if he is to lead.

Motivation. Oswald Chambers observes,

> The motivation must be firstly the command of Jesus . . . the great dominating note is not the needs of men, but the command. Consequently, the real source of inspiration is always behind, never in front. Today, the tendency is to put the inspiration in front . . . to sweep everything in front of us and bring it all out in accordance with our conception of success.[3]

Motivations are tricky. When things are going well, people are happy. But when times are rough, the missionary, pastor, or disciplemaker wonders if he should quit or if he has misunderstood his call from God. He mustn't be misled by circumstances. The command of our Lord, "As you go, make disciples," must be our supreme motivation. His commands are his enablings. Men change, faint, and fall. Alone with God, the leader recharges his spiritual battery by meditating on the example of his victorious Lord.

Good judgment. Wait patiently before God. Get *all* the facts. Get the counsel you need from informed people. Believe the Lord for his wisdom (see James 1:5). Then make a decision with a *whole* heart. God will bless a heart wholly given to discerning and doing his will.

Initiative. Initiative is doing the right thing without waiting to be told. Some people are afraid to try anything. Some Christians wait to be led by the Spirit, afraid they will "get ahead of the Spirit." If you are a child of God, you can be sure of his Spirit's leading (see Romans 8:14). Believe him!

Enthusiasm. Excitement spreads. People catch it. A vision of a mighty God as seen through a leader's life infects the disciple. "Whatsoever thy hand findeth to do, do it with thy might" (Ecclesiastes 9:10). Whatever you do, "do it heartily, as to the Lord, and not unto men; knowing that of the Lord ye shall receive the reward" (Colossians 3:23-24).

J. C. Ryle once wrote,

> Zeal in religion is a burning desire to please God, to do his will, and to advance his glory in the world in every possible way. It is a desire which no man feels by nature—which the Spirit puts in the heart of every believer when he is converted—but which some believers feel so much more strongly than others that they alone deserve to be called "zealous" men. . . . A zealous man in religion is pre-eminently a man of one thing. It is not enough to say that he is earnest, hearty, uncompromising, thorough-going, whole-hearted, fervent in spirit. He only sees one thing, he cares for one thing, he lives

for one thing, he is swallowed up in one thing and that one thing is to please God . . . and to advance God's glory.[4]

A holy zeal is essential to leadership. Christ is our example: "And his disciples remembered that it was written, The zeal of thine house hath eaten me up" (John 2:17).

Flexibility. Experience is a great teacher, but sometimes it can lock us into sterile tradition. Be alert to the possibility that there is always a better way. Openness to the Holy Spirit keeps a man in pace with the world around him. Learn the difference between a principle from God's word and man's methods. The gospel remains the same; human methods change.

Appreciation. The rare art of encouraging someone through genuine praise is a sign of your capacity to love. Give verbal recognition to the energy expended by those around you. A personal letter of appreciation is a rare treasure.

Patience. Jesus was never in a hurry. Quiet actions and words instill confidence in your followers. This single quality of leadership has been more apparent in my observation of leaders than any other single ingredient.

Hurry always implies lack of definite method, confusion, and impatience with slow growth. Hurry seems to make energy a substitute for a clearly defined plan. It is a counterfeit of haste. N. G. Jordon writes, "Everything that is great in life is the product of slow growth; the newer, the greater, and higher, and nobler the work, the slower is its growth, and surer its lasting success."[5]

WHY LEADERS FAIL

According to a recent study, success in leadership is due 15 percent to technical training and skills, and 85 percent to the leader's commitment, experience, and spiritual gifts. The list of major reasons for failure include:

- A lack of initiative
- A lack of ambition
- Carelessness
- An uncooperative spirit
- Laziness

The disciplemaker should analyze his life in light of Scripture, to see if any of these traits are present. "Search me, O God, and know my heart: try me, and know my thoughts: And see if there be any wicked way in me, and lead me in the way everlasting" (Psalm 139:23-24).

WHEN PACESETTING CAN BE DANGEROUS

We run a danger in making too much of one individual or expecting too much of another. Men do fail and will fall. When a member of the church drops out of the fellowship because he sees sin or failing in a leader's life, he is being person-centered rather than Christ-centered.

To avoid this pitfall, we must run the race of life *focusing* on the ultimate pacesetter: "Looking unto Jesus the author and finisher of our faith" (Hebrews 12:2).

Focus on Jesus, but remember that as a pacesetter someone else is focusing on you as his earthly example.

I'd rather see a sermon than hear one any day.
I'd rather one would walk with me than merely show
the way.
The eye's a better pupil and much more willing than
the ear.

Fine counsel is confusing, but example's always clear.
The best of all the teachers are those who live their
creeds.
For to see the good put into action is what everybody
needs.
I'll soon learn how to do it if you'll let me see it done.
I can watch your hand in action, but your tongue too
fast may run.
And the lectures you deliver may be very wise and true,
But I'd rather get my lesson by observing what you do.
For I may misunderstand you in the high advice you
give,
But there's no misunderstanding how you act and how
you live.

Author unknown

QUESTIONS FOR STUDY AND DISCUSSION

1. Why is the "follow-me" principle of the New Testament basically neglected as an operating principle in discipleship ministries today?

2. Why is obedience to Scripture much more demanding than singing, attending services, or listening to lessons and messages?

3. Describe three qualities of a pacesetter which you especially need to develop.

4. Consider the seven leadership qualities for pacesetters.
   a) Which are most important to you?
   b) What would you add to the list and why?

5. Discuss one or more dangers of pacesetting to which you are susceptible.

6. How can one find the balance essential to a "modeling" ministry?

7. Why is a pacesetter essential to train a surgeon, an airplane pilot, or a multiplying disciple?

━━━━━━━━━━━━ NOTES ━━━━━━━━━━━━

1. J. M. Price, *Jesus the Teacher* (Nashville, Tennessee: Sunday School Board, 1946), page 43.

2. Oswald Chambers, *Disciples Indeed* (London: Marshall, Morgan and Scott, 1955), page 10.

3. Oswald Chambers, *So Send I You* (Fort Washington, Pennsylvania: Christian Literature Crusade, 1975), page 74.

4. J. C. Ryle, as quoted in *Knowing God* by J. I. Packer (Downers Grove, Illinois: InterVarsity Press, 1973), pages 156-157.

5. N. G. Jordan, *The Majesty of Calmness* (Old Tappan, New Jersey: Fleming H. Revell Company, 1956), page 17.

PART FOUR

The Practice:
Getting Started Now

CHAPTER ELEVEN

Selecting Potential Multiplying Leaders

*"It's not how many
men, but what
kind of men"*
—Dawson Trotman

DR. HUDSON TAYLOR, founder of the China Inland Mission, had nearly one thousand missionaries, a staggering number, in the interior of China at the turn of the nineteenth century. In one year alone, Taylor's band of laborers lost thirty-eight missionaries and children through death, yet others were ready to take their places.

Many times Dr. Taylor was asked how he recruited so many workers. He replied there were two reasons for this extensive thrust of laborers into China.

Prayer. "Pray ye therefore the Lord of the harvest, that he will send forth labourers into his harvest" (Matthew 9:38). Each year, by faith, Taylor and his colleagues claimed a specific number of new personnel in prayer. God honored their specific intercession.

Lives saturated with the word of God. Dr. Taylor said that to get laborers there must be a deepening of the word of God daily in the lives of lay men and women, so they could not say no to God's call.

These two concepts have revolutionized more than one ministry.

HOW TO FIND POTENTIAL DISCIPLES IN YOUR CHURCH

Looking for a disciple with whom you can share your life is an exciting adventure. Here are some guidelines in how to go about it.

Begin in prayer. The focus of Jesus' prayer strategy in Matthew 9 was for "labourers, reapers, workers, disciples." Cry to God for laborers for the harvest. This is Christ's command. Jesus spent all night in prayer before he chose the twelve (see Luke 6:12).

Look for a hungry person. Dawson Trotman, founder of The Navigators, said we must "find a man who wants God's best for his life and who is willing to pay any price to have it."[1] "Blessed are they which do hunger and thirst after righteousness: for they shall be filled" (Matthew 5:6).

One such individual was a well-educated man named Charlie who wanted answers for his questions about the Bible. His first day in our Sunday school program was the beginning of a new life for Charlie. His teacher was a former missionary who not only answered Charlie's difficult questions from the Bible, but personally visited Charlie to follow him up. They met for six weeks, each week using the Gospel of John studies we used with all our new members.

After this, I began to visit Charlie at his home. I found a hungry man. He had discovered the word in a new way. He began studying the Bible, first one then two hours each evening—personally discovering new treasures in the Scriptures. I took him to visit non-Christians, and Charlie began to win others to Christ.

As he continued to grow spiritually, we asked him to teach a young married men's class. Then he became a deacon. From that questioning, scientific mind came a tender, godly man.

Now people from his classes are scattered all over the world, and at least eight are in full-time ministry. They are reproducing Charlie's life over and over again through spiritual multiplication.

Look for more than a sharp outer appearance. It is difficult to look at a person just with the eyes of faith. We tend to look for a man who has the appearance of a leader. God does not choose on the basis of what we are, however, but on what we can be through his grace. The most unlikely people often become the greatest disciplemakers. "Man looketh on the outward appearance, but the Lord looketh on the heart" (1 Samuel 16:7).

As the apostle Paul viewed the average church members in the first century, he said,

> For ye see your calling, brethren, how that not many wise men after the flesh, not many mighty, not many noble, are called: But God hath chosen the foolish things of the world to confound the wise; and God hath chosen the weak things of the world to confound the things which are mighty; And base things of the world, and things which are despised, hath God chosen, yea, and things which are not, to bring to nought things that are: That no flesh should glory in his presence (1 Corinthians 1:26-29).

We had four workers in our bus ministry who were either slow or retarded, but they were bringing over one hundred children or teens to Sunday school each Sunday! Others in the church who were the poorer members had the most giving hearts. Many with less education spent more time in the ministry of the church than those with impressive academic qualifications. God can get more glory, it sometimes seems, from those who have less to commend themselves.

One of our sons, for example, has been retarded from birth. Yet his faith in Christ and his amazing belief in instant answers to prayer continues to minister to me and challenge me. God uses *both* the weak and the strong. Don't overlook any source of manpower.

Be alert for those who are faithful and able to teach. Only the faithful are eligible for extended personal discipling.

Look for disciples in counseling sessions. One of our church members, Hugh, was having deep sin problems. His marriage was strained. High living, expensive boats, and business pressures had taken their toll on his life. He had little to do with Christ. One of our laymen began counseling Hugh. We had a group which prayed daily for him, and God began turning him around. Slowly he began growing and made a public commitment for Christ. He left a high-paying job, finished college, and attended seminary.

Using their home as a base, Hugh and his wife began a loving ministry and personal discipling of young adults which has produced a constant stream of changed lives. Many young men are in seminary now through Hugh's spiritual multiplication. God used a problem to change a tough heart into a devoted disciplemaker.

Be open to unexpected sources. Some will come to you "out of the blue." These could very well be the ones God sends your way in answer to your prayers for a disciple to train. But remember, if a person is truly hungry, he will take the truth from *any* source you suggest in your church. Watch out for those who want to be instructed only by the pastor or some particular person. Pride may be hindering them.

Take advantage of all group meetings. A Sunday school class is a natural place for finding disciples (remember Edward Kimball's Sunday school outreach). Retreats and conferences give extra momentum through intensive small group interaction and a series of messages on commitment. Concentrated exposure to a Spirit-filled speaker and strong study group leaders will bring church members a long way on the path of discipleship.

Utilize a choice group already serving in the church. Don't overlook the obvious: teachers, deacons, administrators.

Don't ignore family members. We mustn't neglect the most important people in our lives. A father can meet with his teenage son, a mother with the daughter. The home gives more exposure to your life than any other discipling situation. People may ask if you can't develop discipleship in your children, working with them full-time, how can you help others only part-time? Set the pace right at home.

KEY GOALS FOR MULTIPLIERS

When you begin to teach and train others, here are some specific goals to establish for your disciple.

Character development. The quality of life is more important than the quantity of activity in ministry. Is your disciple pure and honest? What are his standards for daily living? If he is mistakenly given wrong change in a store, for example, will he instantly return it? "He that is faithful in that which is least is faithful also in much: and he that is unjust in the least is unjust also in much" (Luke 16:10).

As explained in the chapter on pacesetting, the qualities of the multiplier become a motivating model for the disciple.

Transmitting truth by example is an awesome responsibility. If the original is distinctive, copies of it will be clear also.

A comprehensive viewpoint. Teach the one you are discipling to have a vision for the whole world. He must learn how to reach out beyond his own niche. Pray with him over maps of the city, the state, the nation, and the world. "And ye shall be witnesses unto me both in Jerusalem, and in all Judea, and in Samaria, and unto the uttermost part of the earth" (Acts 1:8). Start at home, but then project and cultivate a vision for reaching the world.

Competence. It was said of Jesus, "He hath done all things well" (Mark 7:37). The modern philosophy is to do as little as we can. The "get-by" syndrome is capturing the church.

Paul wrote, "Not with eye-service, as men-pleasers; but as the servants of Christ, doing the will of God from the heart" (Ephesians 6:6). Set high standards for yourself and your disciple and graciously give your best efforts to the Lord. After a visitation program, witnessing, or any other ministry activity with your disciple, sit down and together evaluate what you have done. With goals, planning, and standards, the growing disciple learns to build *quality* into his ministry.

Consistency. The disciplemaker only has the leverage of love and his own consistent life with which to attract and reach others. Here are some consistent spiritual traits which will draw hungry individuals to your disciples:

- Being Spirit-filled, which results in a positive attitude
- Scripture memorization
- Daily devotional life, which includes Bible study and intercessory prayer
- Personal expression of faith in the home, on the job, and in social settings

Pray to the Lord of the harvest to show you those people

who want to know their Lord better. Begin as soon as possible to develop character, a world vision, competence, and consistency in your disciple.

QUESTIONS FOR STUDY AND DISCUSSION

1. What two ways are suggested by Hudson Taylor to get more "labourers for the harvest" through your church?

2. What can you do now to implement these two ideas in your church ministry?

   Personalize the lesson:
   a) List the names of people in your church who are potential disciples:

   _____
   _____
   _____
   _____
   _____
   _____

   Others _____

   b) Prayerfully narrow your list of people down to five. List their names here. They must be hungry and faithful and able to teach.

   _____
   _____
   _____
   _____
   _____

   c) Now ask the Lord to show you specifically the one or two from this group he would like you to disciple.

═══════════════NOTES═══════════════

1. Dawson Trotman, from a message at a Navigator staff conference, Santa Barbara, California, 1951.

CHAPTER TWELVE

Begin in Your Church Today

*"The church exists
by mission as fire
exists by burning"*
—Emil Brunner

NOTHING THAT LASTS grows overnight. Toadstools grow quickly, but giant redwoods take centuries—the difference in lasting value is indisputable. Building disciples is on the heart of God for his church. It is his plan that the church multiply laborers for the harvest. We need never fear beginning something quietly and on a small scale. God will cause what is his to grow. "If the root be holy, so are the branches" (Romans 11:16).

HOW TO TEACH AND MOTIVATE OTHERS TO MULTIPLY

Since it takes a disciple to build other disciples, the chain of multiplication begins with *you*. Start with only one disciple.

Pour your life into him, using some of the guidelines in this book. As you begin, use these key principles of teaching and motivating:

Tell him why. As you teach your disciple how to pray, for example, tell him why it is important to pray. There are at least fifteen scriptural reasons to pray. Share these with him over a period of time as you pray together.

Show him how. Jesus said, "Follow me," not, "Listen to me." We learn by doing. Words are a poor substitute for a picture. Have you ever read a booklet on "How to Tie Shoelaces"? Imagine constructing the wording to describe the steps.

If you want to encourage your man to study the Bible daily, invite him to meet with you to see how you are doing it. Teach him the "how-tos" of various Bible study methods. Otherwise, he will become tragically dependent upon others for being fed from the Scriptures.

Teach also by exposure. The reason so few people witness is that they have never had a positive soul-winning experience. Your church counseling room should be the most exciting place in the city. Take a prospective counselor-disciple into this marvelous experience. Show him how to lead someone to Christ. Take him with you into a home and let him share in your witness until he is able to lead another to Christ.

Get him started. Give your disciple specific assignments. He needs to know they are ones which you have done or are presently doing. Because you have been pacesetting with high standards, he will be expected to complete his work with excellence.

Let him know that if he has a problem with the project, you are a resource person who will help him in any way you can.

Call him during the week. Intensify your personal relationship with him. Be available to him. The gospel wouldn't have been taken into the Roman world and beyond if Christ had formalized and limited his disciples' access to him.

Keep him going. Check the assignment. Follow-up is important. There is nothing more disappointing to a young disciple than to have worked hard all during the week and then have you give his effort only a cursory glance when you get together. People are more attentive to their work when they know it will be inspected.

A teacher at the Narramore Foundation was assigned the teaching responsiblity for grade school misfits and problem children. Praying carefully about each child, this unusual teacher committed herself to write a complimentary note daily to each child on some aspect of his or her work. Sometimes it was a challenge to write even one sentence for the harder cases, but this caring teacher always found something constructive to say. Gradually, her class was transformed into a miracle. Some children saved their notes for the whole year.

Learning is increased through a positive reward system. It is easy for anyone to pick another person to pieces, but it takes inspiration from the Holy Spirit and love to compliment a person sincerely for the good job he's done.

To motivate as you teach, accept a person totally. "As in water face answereth to face, so the heart of man to man" (Proverbs 27:19). We can't hide an unaccepting attitude. This does not mean we *approve* of everything a person does in order to accept him totally. Christ accepted us, loving us to the uttermost; yet all our sins were before him (see John 13:1 and Romans 5:6-8).

Show your acceptance by listening intently. Keep quiet and let another talk. You will learn much!

Affirm your disciple. Don't let a know-it-all attitude on your part tear him down.

113

When we were first married, my wife would come to me with her Bible study and enthusiastically show me a new truth she had just discovered. Sometimes I would say, "I'm glad you found it, dear; but I discovered that twelve years ago while researching a Greek verb." Oops! I killed her joy on the spot.

I've since learned to show excitement when she shares the Scriptures with me. I also check my own application of her discovery and talk it over with her. In this way she is encouraged and I learn as well.

My own need for encouragement has been met many times as I've done character studies of Bible people, seeing God's amazing grace in their lives. Reading biographies also provides an excellent source of encouragement through God's supernatural ability to use ordinary people for his glory.

Teach him to multiply. Keep the goal of spiritual multiplication constantly before his eyes. Along with methods and materials from the Bible, teach him also how to pass on what he learns to the disciples he will eventually be reaching.

WORKING DISCIPLESHIP TRAINING INTO YOUR CHURCH

Here are several avenues through which you can lead your church into extensive training of disciples.

1. Use the existing church structures and group organizations such as Sunday school classes and church training sessions.

2. Use visitation evangelism to link the man you are training in discipleship with the lost. This becomes a major source of multiplication.

3. Use retreats and conferences. Through a number of

one- or two-day retreats each year, God will move potential disciples into the commitments essential for the next step in growth toward multiplication.

4. The pastor has a vital role in discipling. He should be a model for others in the church to follow. Pray faithfully for your pastor's spiritual growth. Leadership building should be a priority in the pastor's own ministry. He can begin discipling his staff, his deacons or board of elders, and should also be meeting regularly with one or two laymen.

5. The individuals who are discipling others should meet together for monthly progress reports. The future growth of the church and the preparation of leaders is more dependent upon this group's influence than upon any other single group within the congregation. Pray by name for all those who are being influenced in the discipling ministry. During the month, watch for positive experiences which can be shared at this meeting as encouragement. Review Christ's command to disciple the nations. Pray that God will call people from your church into home and foreign mission groups.

Chart the progress of your discipling ministry by drawing your church's multiplication chains on a chalkboard. Keep watch for the fourth generation fruit, the "others also" of 2 Timothy 2:2. Make much of those investing their lives in one or two people.

GET STARTED NOW!

Begin by choosing a potential multiplier, after much prayer. He must be faithful and able to teach. Have a series of six meetings with assignments on the basics. If he shows further interest, then meet for a period of up to six months. You will soon learn if God is using you to minister in his life—and if he is a potential multiplier.

Meet regularly with the person you are discipling. This consistent time is invaluable for gauging a person's pace in Christ. It takes time to get to know someone well. Time of day is not as important as regular meetings.

Select a neutral location, which is quiet enough for you to talk and pray together without interruptions or phone calls or other distractions.

An hour is average for sharing, checking the assignment, prayer, and teaching new material. Beware of spending all the time solving problems. Some of this will be essential, but you may have to set another time devoted to such difficulties if they start eating up your hour. The basis of your training time in a man-to-man ministry is an emphasis on nurturing growth and the application of Scripture to life. However, discipling doesn't end with the hour. Commit yourself to be available to lift and lead the disciple over a longer period of time.

Work with only one or two people per year in personal discipling. Let your multiplication happen from that small start. It works faster than you think. In six months there are two of you; four in a year. Then eight, sixteen, thirty-two, and sixty-four in just three years. If you have gone for three years in spiritual life *without any multiplication whatsoever*, just think what you could have done—think about what you can now begin to do! Your spiritual descendants can soon reach to the uttermost parts of the earth!

Maintain your other group training ministries even while concentrating on one disciple; you just won't be able to train a group as specifically and intensively as you will your single disciple.

Begin a plan of personal Bible study which you will do with your disciple. Stay at least one step ahead, for then you can anticipate his questions and problems. You will be a model and pacesetter he can follow.

116

Make use of all the excellent materials available today that are designed to enrich and encourage personal discipling. Remember though, that it is the man rather than the materials that is God's focus. The list of materials at the end of this chapter provides many sources which have been successfully and widely used to help people grow through individual and group discipling.

Involve the disciple in personal evangelism. Read the book of Acts together. Have him prepare his testimony and practice giving it to you, then go out. Initially, do the witnessing yourself, showing him how; then progressively, let him do it. Take time for church and neighborhood visitation. Many future spiritual generations will be the direct product of the discipler's commitment to share an hour a week with his disciple in direct evangelism.

Remind the team of disciples God gives to you that their goal is to penetrate every stratum of the church with the love of Christ. Help them to apply personally the practical truths of 1 Thessalonians 5:12-25 to the total church life. Growth will occur. Others will be drawn into the fellowship of loving concern and discipline, and the multiplication of Christ's life will continue.

We have learned how to pick potential multipliers through prayer and lives saturated with the word of God. We have reviewed the many places where you can find disciples, including your own family, and have recognized that ordinary, weak people can be used by God. We have discussed the qualities of character, comprehensive viewpoint, competence, and consistency which should be built into a disciple's life.

Hungry hearts want all the Lord has for them in life. They are willing to pay the price through suffering, love, study, and discipline. Are *you* willing to pay the price to get spiritual food and then give it away?

QUESTIONS FOR STUDY AND DISCUSSION

1. For each of the five steps in teaching outlined for this chapter, describe one concrete example which you can implement.

2. What motivated you in your early Christian life? What is the most effective motivating influence in your life now?

3. What motivational tools are being used to encourage people in your Sunday school or church?

4. What could you do to encourage at least one person in a more personal walk with Christ?

5. Discuss the role of Barnabas as a motivator and encourager in the life of John Mark and Paul (see Acts 4:36-37; 9:26-28; 11:22-26; 13:1-3; 15:25-26, 35-41).

6. How would you characterize the New Testament as a motivational tool for today? Share some of the Scriptures that have motivated you.

7. How could you insert a motivating message on discipleship or disciplemaking into your Sunday school, preaching services, or other church programs?

8. Discuss the significance (advantages, effects) of beginning with one or two people rather than a large group.

MATERIALS TO ENCOURAGE SPIRITUAL GROWTH

Christ in You. Downers Grove, Illinois: InterVarsity Press, 1979.

Coleman, Lyman. *Serendipity Bible Studies Series.* Waco, Texas: Word Publishers, 1979.

Cosgrove, Francis M. *Essentials of Discipleship.* Colorado Springs, Colorado: NavPress, 1980.

Design for Discipleship. Colorado Springs, Colorado: Nav-Press, 1980.

Discovery I: A Guide to Christian Growth. San Bernardino, California: Here's Life Publishers, 1975.

Grow Your Christian Life. Downer's Grove, Illinois: InterVarsity Press, 1979.

Growing in Christ. Colorado Springs, Colorado: NavPress, 1980.

Klein, Chuck. *So You Want Solutions.* Wheaton, Illinois: Tyndale House Publishers, 1979.

Lord, Peter. *2959 Plan.* Titisville, Florida: Park Avenue AGAPE Ministries, 1976.

Miller, Chuck. *Now That I'm a Christian.* Vol. 1 and 2. Glendale, California: Regal Press, 1979.

Moore, Waylon. *Building Disciples Notebook.* Tampa, Florida: Missions Unlimited, Inc., 1978.

Myra, Harold. *The New You.* Wheaton, Illinois: Victor Books/Scripture Press, 1972.

Neighbors, Ralph W. *Survivial Kit for New Christians.* Nashville, Tennessee: Convention Press, 1979.

Pratney, Winkie. *A Handbook for Followers of Jesus.* Minneapolis, Minnesota: Bethany Fellowship, 1976.

Ten Basic Steps to Christian Maturity. Arrowhead Springs, California: Campus Crusade for Christ, 1968.

Willis, Avery. *Masterlife Notebook.* Nashville, Tennessee: Convention Press, 1980.

CHAPTER THIRTEEN

Anyone Can Multiply

*"You are giving
yourself for some-
thing—what are you
getting in exchange
for your life?"*
—Roy Robertson

ANYONE CAN DISCIPLE others. That's what this book is all
about. And a disciplemaking ministry can be launched right
in your local church.

We started with an account of the multiplication chain of
a Sunday school teacher. We will end with a story about
another Sunday school teacher—one who influenced me and
started my chains of spiritual multiplication.

When I was ten years old, my Sunday school class had a
succession of teachers. We were a tough group to handle!
The newest teacher, prim Mrs. Wallen, was in her fifties and
looked like easy prey to us. We easily destroyed her first
lesson.

But she changed all that quickly. She visited me and asked
if I could help her keep the class quiet so they could hear the

Bible. She had probably visited each of the class members with the same request, for next Sunday things were much quieter, and we began to hear the gospel. She made Jesus so real that all of us were converted that first year. Those who lastingly affect others for Christ seem to have this ability to make him real to others.

Shortly before her death, Mrs. Wallen told me she had prayed for each of her boys by name for over thirty-eight years. She knew where they all were and how they were serving the Lord. Imagine how many chains of multiplying disciples she started—right in her Sunday school class!

Another ordinary Christian who affected my own spiritual growth was Bruce Miller. I was attending the law school at Baylor University when I met Bruce. He was in my speech class. I had little in common with this "preacher boy," yet it seemed as if I was always bumping into Bruce. We would talk for a few minutes, and I would always leave his presence with a burning heart. The Lord was working on me through him. I began trying to dodge Bruce, but he seemed to find me anyway.

I shared with him about the trauma caused by my father's death and my mother's serious illness. I told him my little sister was living with relatives, my younger brother was already out on his own, and I was no longer excited about pursuing the legal profession. The love and concern Bruce showed me during those trying days won me over.

Praying for me, sharing the word with me, and living a disciplined spiritual life before me, Bruce was used of God to bring me to a place of total commitment to Christ. It was during those last months at the university that God called me into the ministry. My life's direction changed forever. It wasn't until later that I realized that what Bruce had done with me and was doing with others was *standard New Testament discipling*. He was doing the things described in this book.

While at seminary I began praying in a new way. At a conference I heard Dawson Trotman, founder of The Navigators, describe how years before he had specifically prayed for each state in the United States, then for many foreign countries. He asked God to do three things: to raise up national workers, to send out missionaries to train the nationals, and to use him personally in each of the countries he prayed for.

I borrowed this vision as my prayer. In my small room near the campus I would kneel over a map of the world and pray. I sometimes felt foolish as I put my finger on the names of the capital cities of foreign countries.

Not everything was going well in my personal life at that time. I had no steady work. It seemed that pulpit committees didn't want to consider a young, untried preacher. But God was using those days to smooth my rough edges and enlarge my vision. I became totally convinced that my prayers for the lost world would be answered.

God soon opened my eyes to hungry-hearted men everywhere. I learned much, though I made many mistakes in trying to help others. Eventually, I pastored a country church and a city mission, spending personal time with anyone who would give me the opportunity. I did with them what Bruce had done with me. Souls were won and lives changed.

Years later I designed a series of simple Bible studies for the radio ministry of Pacific Garden Mission in Chicago. The six lessons on the Gospel of John which were designed to help follow up new Christians began to have an effect. In fact, within a year people from every state and nine foreign countries wrote that they had trusted Christ through those Bible studies! Their testimonies were the answers to those hours of prayer on the floor with my map. And this was just the beginning.

I met a tall west Texas youth named Max. He had a heart for witnessing, and I encouraged him in his ministry of evangelism to the students at Texas A and M University. We spent hours together over the years as I discipled Max and prayed for him. Just last year, while visiting Thailand and Indonesia, I met student workers who said, "You are my spiritual great-grandfather!" We traced the chain of spiritual multiplication back to Max. Now Max Barnett is the Student Director of the Baptist Student Union's campus ministry at the University of Oklahoma, which has a world-wide outreach.

Discipling gets better as the years go by because it gets richer in production through multiplication. For a period of time I was helping a mechanic who had a sixth-grade education, an engineer, some seminary students, a Bible school student, and Max. All of the seminary students eventually went to the mission field—Mexico, Panama, Vietnam, Indonesia, Brazil, and Barbados. The mechanic became an active deacon and spiritual leader in his church. The engineer went into teaching so he could have more direct time with individuals whom he could disciple.

Does this work in the church? It certainly does! The pulpit is not only for teaching and evangelism; it is also a point from which to net hungry hearts in whose lives the Lord is at work.

Early in my pastorate at a large city church, I asked the congregation if there were any men who would like to meet with me the next morning in my office at 6:00 in order to begin studying the Bible in depth. The group never averaged more than eight men, but over the months they grew spiritually. They developed self-feeding habits that revolutionized their lives. Most of them were elected deacons, teachers, and department directors in the church. From that study group, I prayerfully selected two each year to whom I would give more intensive, personal, one-to-one discipling time.

Out of the ministry with these select men came most of the twenty-five people from our church who went into full-time Christian service. Four others went to the mission field. And hundreds were won to Christ year after year by this group. We were baptizing an average of one hundred people each year for thirteen years.

The laymen then began training others in counseling and follow-up in neighboring churches (a ministry which is continuing today). Now our city is ringed with pastors and church staff who made their initial commitment to the ministry through these small group Bible studies and individual discipling ministries.

The Lord continues to answer another part of my prayers. I constantly receive invitations from overseas to share follow-up principles and discipleship training. I have spoken in over thirty nations, and I've taught individuals from more than eighty nations.

Any disciple can multiply his life in Christ by applying the biblical principles in his local church. From your church God will send out men and women who will disciple the nations. Ask him and believe him.

May I share a prayer with you as you begin this week to pray for someone you can disciple? "The Lord God of your fathers make you a thousand times so many more as ye are, and bless you, as he hath promised you!" (Deuteronomy 1:11).

QUESTIONS FOR STUDY AND DISCUSSION

1. Who has been most influential in helping you develop your spiritual life? Check one or two.

— Mother
— Father
— Sunday school teacher
— Pastor
— Student worker or church staff person
— Relative
— Friend
— Acquaintance
— Other

2. How did these individuals influence you?

3. Would your spiritual life be any different today if follow-up or individual discipling had begun immediately after your conversion?

4. If someone did follow you up or disciple you, how did they go about it?

5. What needs to be done to encourage your Sunday school to become more involved in follow-up and discipling?

6. Whom are you now influencing spiritually? Name someone from one of the following categories:
   — Home
   — Work
   — School
   — Church

7. Whom are you praying for daily? As you pray for them, ask the following questions:
   a) What is their deepest need?
   b) What is my part in meeting this need?
   c) What is the first step in doing my part?

Appendix

INDIVIDUAL AND GROUP DISCIPLING

Producing leadership is a critical unmet need in the local church. Training in a group can be a starting point for developing leaders, but it has some limitations. However, personal discipling one to one includes the personal involvement and commitment of time necessary to train leaders effectively. A biblical discipling relationship should become a lifetime commitment to intercession and encouragement as the one we disciple grows.

Which one? Group or individual ministry? It is not either/or, but both. Individual discipling is not a restrictive relationship. The same people can be involved in both ministries.

REASONS FOR INDIVIDUAL DISCIPLING

1. Anyone in the local church can do individual discipling. He simply shares with another what the Lord is doing in his life, and leads the other in the step which he has already taken.

2. Individual ministry is modeled in the church by personal counseling to the lost, sick, bereaved, discouraged, and those with expressed needs. It is equally logical to give quality time to people who desire spiritual growth.

3. Christ's ministry was to love his disciples and lay down his life for them (see John 13:1). Working with an individual captures the commitment of Christ to each of his men.

4. Few people have the time or capacity to be intimately involved in the lives of a number of individuals. Anyone can make time for working with one person.

5. Individual discipling has the closeness of friendship and the precision of an apprentice relationship.

6. It is flexible in scheduling, time frame, Bible study assignments, and training. These can be changed or paced according to individual needs. Spiritual growth is more rapid.

7. This method of individual discipling is readily copied. We do unto others what has been done unto us.

8. Exhortation, correction, and admonition are quickly and easily given in the setting of individual discipling.

9. The life of the discipler reinforces the truth of the message, and is in close view of the disciple.

10. The needs of the disciple surface in the privacy of individual ministry.

11. Both the relationship and the results seem more lasting in individual discipling.

12. Discipling on a one-to-one level is the most rapid way I know to develop spiritual leaders who can multiply disciples.

REASONS FOR GROUP DISCIPLING

1. Group ministry is the most-used method in the local church. People feel at home with it and expect its methodology.

2. It is a fluid method. An individual can move in and out of

a group without destroying either the group or his or her relationship with those attending.

3. It allows people to participate without feeling put on the spot. Some people are not ready for one-to-one discipling.

4. A variety of teaching methods can be used in the group setting.

5. General doctrine can be easily taught to several people at once, with a time saving to the instructor.

6. Bible study is highly stimulating as many share together their research and application.

7. Momentum can grow in groups. A spirit of adventure and unity can motivate others less interested over a period of time.

8. The effect of general correction and exhortation is more subtle than direct confrontation.

9. A group counseling effect can result from people becoming interested in and praying for the needs of others.

10. Groups are effective channels for funneling people into a more intensive one-to-one relationship and training time.

11. The Holy Spirit can use the background and experiences of a number of people to teach others.

12. Spiritual gifts that minister to individuals can be balanced with the gifts of others for group strength and ministry.